EVIDENCE PROBLEMS

EVIDENCE PROBLEMS

Bruce G. Berner
Valparaiso University Law School

NATIONAL INSTITUTE FOR TRIAL ADVOCACY

Address inquiries to:

Reprint Permission
National Institute for Trial Advocacy
1685 38th Street, Suite 200
Boulder, CO 80301-2735
Phone: (800) 225-6482
Fax: (720) 890-7069
E-mail: permissions@nita.org

ISBN 978-1-60156-429-0
FBA 1429

Library of Congress Cataloging-in-Publication Data

Berner, Bruce G., author.

  Evidence problems / Bruce G. Berner, Valparaiso University Law School.

     pages cm

  ISBN 978-1-60156-429-0

1. Evidence (Law)--United States.--Problems, exercises, etc. I. Title.

  KF8935.Z9B475 2014

  347.73'6--dc23

                                        2014023771

Printed in the United States.

. Wolters Kluwer

Official co-publisher of NITA.
WKLegaledu.com/NITA

Contents

Contents

SECTION A

PROBLEMS FOR CLASSROOM ASSIGNMENT

Many of the problems in Section A are based on events in this story. When such is true, the problem number is followed by the letter "S" to indicate it is based on the story. When no "S" appears, the problem is self-standing. Most of the people in the problem are fictitious; the roadside accident scenario is loosely based on *Derdiarian v. Felix Contracting Corp.*, 414 N.E.2d 666 (N.Y. 1980).

RORY CROOT'S LONG DAY

The following events all occur in the Nita City, largest city and capital of the State of Nita, a little-known state in the United States. Nita is in the mainstream of American law and has adopted completely the Federal Rules of Evidence for state proceedings. It is in the District of Nita, part of the Fourteenth Circuit.

Walter Workman is employed by "Tar Is Us," a company subcontracting for "Roads Are Us," the contractor for repair of State Highway 49 under contract with the State of Nita Highway Department. Roads Are Us is legally responsible for all safety issues both for motorists and workers in the construction area. One morning, Diana Driver is proceeding north on Highway 49 in her 2013 National Motors car. She is approaching the construction area taking her two children, Donny and Deena, to school when her car skids off the road, breaks through a small wooden sawhorse placed for the protection of workers, and slams into a huge vat of tar that spills onto Walter, injuring him. Deena is hurt when the rear window in Diana's car explodes as the car hits the vat. Young police officer, Rory Croot, is called to the scene to investigate and, after talking to many eyewitnesses, including the pedestrian passerby Ernie Augen, files an official accident report. Subsequently, Walter files a civil action for damages against Diana and Roads Are Us. He also files a worker's compensation claim against Tar Is Us. Deena, through Diana as guardian *ad litem,* files a product liability action against National Motors alleging a manufacturing defect in the glass in the rear window.

As Rory is finishing his work and Walter is taken away in an ambulance, Rory gets a call to proceed quickly to the Nickel & Dime Savings Bank to help with an ongoing robbery. A bit earlier, two masked men had entered the bank and, brandishing guns, had forced Tammy Cassiere to place $10,000 into bags for them and then ran out. A description of the men was put out over the police radio, and, as Rory approaches to within three blocks of the bank, he sees men who meet the description running away from the bank with a large bag. He arrests them and determines that their names are Tom and Jerry. During a "pat down" of the arrestees, Rory discovers cocaine in Tom's pocket. Subsequently, the prosecutor charges Tom and Jerry with robbery and conspiracy to commit robbery, and charges Tom with possession of a controlled substance.

After a long day of processing, booking, and jailing the arrestees, interviewing witnesses at the bank, and filing a report, Rory is nearly finished with his shift when he passes the downtown brewpub, Bruce and Barb's Place. He sees a young man who appears to Rory to be about fifteen years old sitting at a table by the window drinking a beer. He enters, asks to see the youth's ID, and the youth shows him an ID that Rory immediately recognizes as fake. After a few minutes, the boy gives his real ID to Rory that shows that he is Sam Boire and is sixteen years of age. Rory arrests him for underage drinking and files a report. A juvenile delinquency proceeding is commenced against Sam.

On Rory's way home, he stops at Bruce and Barb's Place and has a microbrew called Nita City Beer.

Relevancy

Rule 401

[handwritten: ① What fact are we trying to prove? — chain of reasoning]

Discuss whether the following items of evidence are relevant or irrelevant under the definition in Rule 401. [Do not consider any effect that Rule 403 or any other rule might have on the admissibility of the evidence. This problem is strictly about basic relevancy under Rule 401.]

1S. An Walter's worker's compensation action against Tar Is Us, the defendant *[handwritten: → FACT]* introduces testimony that Walter was not paying close attention when he was hit and that, had he been, he probably could have avoided any injury.
[handwritten: Irrelevant - fails materiality b/c Workers Comp cont. neg. doesn't matter]

2. *State v. Donald* for the murder of Victor Timm. Donald stipulates that Timm's death was due to a gunshot. The prosecution calls Dr. Sharif, the county medical examiner, to testify that his autopsy listed the cause of Timm's death as "gunshot." *[handwritten: Relevant - cause of death is material to a murder trial]*

3. *P v. D.* Assume it is material for P to prove that X was in Chicago during a given four-hour period of time on June 15, YR-1. To prove this, P calls Armand, owner and operator of "Armand's Bar & Grille" in Islamabad, Pakistan, to testify that during that same four-hour block of time (after correcting for time difference, of course) Armand was hosting at his Bar & Grille and that X was not present during that time. *[handwritten: Example as to how low the bar is for relevancy]*
[handwritten: Relevant - location makes it a tiny bit more likely he was in Chicago]

4S. In Walter's action against Diana and Roads Are Us, Diana introduces the testimony of Walter's coworker, Steve, that Walter was sleeping on the ground by the vat at the time of the accident. *[handwritten: Relevant - negligence tort material to cont. negligence]*

5S. Testimony of Walter's coworker, Jack, that five minutes before the accident, Jack saw Walter sleeping on the ground by the vat. *[handwritten: Relevant - negligence tort material to contributory negligence]*

6S. Walter's suit against Diana includes damages for an injured back. Diana offers testimony that Walter had a preexisting back injury. *[handwritten: Relevant - damages]*

7S. Testimony of Frank Seguidor, who was in the car behind Diana, that Diana's car had swerved onto the shoulder twice in two miles before they reached the construction site. *[handwritten: Relevant - more likely she swerved again]*

8S. Testimony that Diana is carrying $8 million in automobile liability insurance. *[handwritten: Relevant - more/less likely Diana would drive safely]*

9S. Testimony that Diana has owned a fashionable boutique in downtown Nita City for the last ten years. Relevant - basic biographical info can be relevant to jury seeing the "whole" person

10S. Testimony that Ernie Augen was not wearing his contact lenses that morning when he witnessed the accident. Relevant - credibility of witness testimony always relevant

11S. Testimony that as Diana approached the construction site, her son Donny was yelling at her to go back home because Donny had left his science-fair project at home and it was due that day. Relevant - more likely she was distracted/negligent

12S. Testimony offered by the prosecution that Trixie, a witness called by Tom in the controlled substances trial, is living with Tom. Relevant - witness credibility less likely to be credible

13S. Testimony of Cantare, an officer with the Police Department Internal Affairs Division, that Rory had been disciplined in the past for planting controlled substances on arrestees. Relevant - less likely Δ was in possession

14S. At Jerry's trial for robbery, evidence that Jerry had been convicted twelve years ago for robbery. Relevant - more likely he's robbed again

15S. Testimony offered against Roads Are Us of Rod Byggmester, an expert in road construction design, that the absence of flagmen and the reliance solely on a sawhorse rather than heavy equipment between the roadway and the vat of tar is well below the custom in the industry and the best practices manual for road construction published by an engineering trade association; it is further his opinion that the sawhorse was insufficient. Relevant - more likely Roads Are Us was negligent

16S. To prove that Jerry robbed the Nickel & Dime Savings Bank, prosecution offers the testimony of Pete Walker, who would testify that at 11:15 a.m. (a few minutes after the time of the robbery), he saw Jerry running away from the bank. Relevant - more likely he robbed the bank

EXCLUSION OF RELEVANT EVIDENCE

[handwritten annotation: 1) what fact does ——→ what fact does it make more or less likely / this evidence go / to proving/disproving?]

RULE 403

[handwritten annotation: 2) danger of unfair prejudice or waste of time?]

In each case, indicate the probative value of the evidence, the grounds for possible exclusion under Rule 403 (the "trial concern"), and predict whether the judge would allow the evidence.

1S. Walter introduces testimony that two minutes before the accident, Diana's son, Donny, said to Diana, "Oh, no, Mom! My science fair project is due today, and I left it at home!" *[handwritten: probative value outweighs risk of unfair prejudice & potential time waste]*

2S. Walter introduces testimony that immediately thereafter, Deena said, "Tough, Donny. It's your own darn fault. Don't make me late because of your mistake," and that a wrestling match in the backseat ensued. *[handwritten: probative value outweighs risk of unfair prejudice or waste of time]*

3S. Testimony that Walter's breakfast that morning had been a can of Bud Light. *[handwritten: probative value outweighs risk of unfair prejudice]*

4S. Plaintiff offers a color photograph of Walter lying on the ground covered with tar with burn marks clearly visible on his face and neck. Another twenty-five photos are offered that show Walter wearing only a pair of gym shorts after a series of skin-graft operations. *[handwritten: probative value outweighs unfair prejudice but maybe not for all 25 photos - cumulative argument to exclude some]*

5S. Same as question 4S except that the defendants agree to stipulate that Walter was burned and required skin grafts.

6. *P v. D.* Assume it is material for P to prove that X was in Chicago during a given four-hour period of time on June 15, YR-1. To prove this, P calls Armand, owner and operator of Armand's Bar & Grille in Islamabad, Pakistan, to testify that during that same four-hour block of time (after correcting for time difference, of course) Armand was hosting in his Bar & Grille and that X was not present during that time. *[handwritten: waste of time outweighs probative value]*

7S. Assume that the main rival of the Nita City's baseball team, "The Saints," is the team from a neighboring state, "The Sinners." The Sinners are <u>deeply hated</u> by most Nita City residents. Tammy Cassiere states that one of the robbers was wearing a Sinners baseball hat. To connect him to the robbery, the prosecution offers testimony that when Jerry was arrested, he was wearing a Sinners hat. [Assume it has been shown that approximately 10,000 Sinners hats have been sold to residents of Nita.] *[handwritten right margin: - risk of unfair prejudice]* *[handwritten: probative value outweighs unfair prejudice but Δ will want to bring up 10,000 hats argument]*

8S. The prosecution introduces evidence at Tom's trial for possession of a controlled substance that he was twice previously convicted for possession of controlled substances. *risk of unfair prejudice outweighs probative value - prior bad acts generally excluded as character evidence*

9S. Assume that Sam is waived to adult criminal court and charged with "Minor in Possession" of alcohol. The prosecution calls ten of Sam's friends to testify that he was in Bruce and Barb's Place that day and was drinking beer.

all 10 would risk waste of time / cummulative evidence over probative value

Competency of Lay Witnesses

Rules 601–606; Rule 615

1S. Ernie Augen needs contacts to see clearly. He did not have his contacts in at the time he witnessed the accident. Is he competent to testify to what he saw?

2S. Other problems are brought out about Ernie on voir dire. He is a heroin addict, was convicted two years ago for perjury, takes money *out* of the offering plate at his church, and stole the shoes of two nuns last week. Is Ernie competent to testify?

3S. Walter calls coworker Cliff to testify. Cliff refuses to take an oath because he does not believe in God. He is, however, willing to affirm that he will tell the truth. May he testify?

4S. Roads Are Us calls Walter's foreman, George, to testify. George is a winner of the Nobel Peace Prize, was a professor of philosophy at Nita State University, and is chair of the board of elders at his church. When asked if he promises to tell the truth, George says: "What is truth anyway? Who can know for sure the ways of God and man? I cannot promise to tell the truth without answers to these profound philosophical questions." Is George competent to testify?

5S. Coworker Cliff testifies that while he was working, when the accident happened, he thinks he saw Diana's car leave the road and that she was turned around and facing the back seat at that time, though he is not positive. Is Cliff competent to testify in this manner?

6S. Larry Anwalt, attorney for Walter, spoke with Percy Verr, another eyewitness to the accident, months prior to the trial. Percy told Larry that he saw the accident and that Diana was not paying attention to her driving when her car ran off the road. On direct examination, when Larry asks Percy if he noticed whether Diana was paying attention, Percy testifies, "Oh, yes, she was paying very close attention." Larry then asks if Percy remembers telling Larry the opposite during an interview. Percy says, "No, I never said any such thing, you liar!" Can Larry testify to Percy's statement during the interview?

7S. At the robbery trial of Tom and Jerry, Tom has indicated on his witness list that he plans to call Al Ibby as a witness. The prosecution moves that Al and all other defense witnesses (except for Tom and Jerry themselves) be excluded from witnessing the trial until they have testified. Tom and Jerry object. How should the court rule?

DIRECT EXAMINATION
(COMPELLING ATTENDANCE, LEADING QUESTIONS, REFRESHING RECOLLECTION)

1S.   About a month before the trial, the parties all learn that Ernie Augen is moving to Hawaii in a week. What options are available to obtain his attendance at the trial or otherwise preserve his testimony?

2S.   Assume a party learns of Ernie's move after it occurs, but needs his testimony. What options are available?

3S.   On direct examination, Walter asks Connie, a coworker who has just testified that she saw Diana's car swerve off the road, "Was her car going about forty mph at that time?" Diana objects that this is a leading question. What is the correct ruling?

4S.   On direct examination of Tammy Cassiere, the prosecutor asks, "Did the men who robbed you act nervous?" Tom and Jerry object that this is an improper leading question. What is the correct ruling?

5S.   Assume that Sam Boire has been waived to adult court and is on trial for "Consumption of Alcohol by a Minor." The prosecution calls his girlfriend, Gidget, who has been going steady with Sam for three years, and begins the direct examination with pointed, leading questions. Sam objects. What result?

6S.   On cross-examination of Gidget, Sam's counsel asks, "Isn't it true that Sam was drinking a root beer when arrested that day?" Prosecution objects that this is an improper leading question. What result?

7S.   Diana calls Donny. When her attorney asks Donny what time they started out for school that morning, Donny said, "About four o'clock." [Actually, as the attorney well knows, it was about eight o'clock.] What options are available to Diana's counsel to correct this error?

8S.   When Rory talked to Barb at the brewpub, Barb stated that she had served Sam a glass of Nita Light Ale, a beer from a local microbrewery. Rory reported that statement in his report. When the prosecution calls Barb and asks what she served Sam, Barb said, "I don't remember. So many people were there that day." How can the prosecution attempt to refresh Barb's recollection?

Hearsay: Basic Definition

Rule 801(a)–(c)

In each of the following problems, indicate whether the testimony is hearsay within the definition of Rule 801(a)–(c). Do not address the question of whether the testimony is ultimately admissible, but only whether it is hearsay. Consider no objection other than hearsay. If the question states what the testimony is offered to prove, assume that is its only purpose. If nothing is stated, consider the question based on various possible uses for which such testimony might be offered.

1S. Parry Notfall, one of the EMS team responding to a call about Walter's injuries, takes the stand and is questioned by Walter's counsel about what Ernie Augen reported to Parry about Walter's actions (and inactions) the ten minutes between the event and the arrival of the EMS team.
declarant ← *declarant's statement depends on declarant's truthfulness - hearsay*

2S. Parry Notfall states that Ernie Augen wrote out a statement on paper and clipboard supplied by Parry. Walter's counsel asks Parry to read that statement.
hearsay but written

3S. Same as question 2S except Ernie's statement was notarized by Nancy Greffier, a notary who just happened to be at the scene with her stamp and seal.
still hearsay

4S. To prove the truth of what Ernie Augen said, Ernie is called to the stand and asked what he told Parry Notfall. *hearsay - out-of-court statement*
asking what he saw would eliminate the hearsay problem

5S. To prove that it was warm on the day Walter was injured, Walter introduces the testimony of Ernie Augen, which states that all the workers and others at the scene were wearing short-sleeve shirts. *not hearsay*
no assertion by wearing short-sleeves — statement made in court

6S. To prove that Jerry was one of the bank robbers, Rory would testify that Jerry was running away from the bank when he first saw him.
not hearsay - testifying what he saw - running away is not an assertion

7S. To prove that Jerry was one of the bank robbers, prosecution calls Tammy Cassiere, who would testify that at a lineup conducted the next day, when asked if she could identify the men who robbed the bank, she pointed at Tom and Jerry.
hearsay - pointing asserts guilt of T & J - out of court

8S. To impeach Ernie Augen's testimony that he saw the collision, Diana calls Ernie's friend, Bert, who would testify that later that same day, Ernie told Bert, "I was walking by an accident scene this morning and heard loud noises, but didn't turn around to look until the whole event was over."
not hearsay - used to impeach

9S. To impeach Ernie Augen, Diana introduces a three-year-old conviction of Ernie for perjury. *hearsay b/c the statement (conviction) depends on the truth of the record - evidentiary value exists only if the record is correct → admissible b/c of exemption*

National Institute for Trial Advocacy

10. *State v. Dewey* is a prosecution for battery of Farragut. Dewey raises the defense of "defense of others," claiming that he shoved Farragut because he thought Farragut was about to hit Dewey's son. To prove that he was reasonable in so thinking, Dewey's counsel puts Dewey on the stand to testify that "The day before the incident, my friend, Fred, told me that Farragut has a long history of hitting small boys." *not hearsay - state of mind*

11. To prove that Viswanathan Anand (current world chess champion) can speak English [assume relevancy], the plaintiff offers a video of a man [authenticated to be Viswanathan] giving a brilliant lecture in English on the Giuoco Piano, a famous chess opening.

12. *Priscilla Lehrer v. Nita School of Law* is a civil action for improper firing of a tenured employee. Defendant's defense is that one of the grounds for releasing a tenured employee—"incompetence"—justified its action. To prove her competence, Priscilla introduces a letter from the Harvard Law School dated last week offering her a tenured appointment at Harvard for $1 million per year starting next August. *not hearsay ~~impeachment~~ circumstantial evidence of competance (ltr doesn't assert competance)*

13. *State v. Tyson* is a criminal action for bestiality with a chicken. To prove Tyson's propensity, the prosecution offers magazines found in Tyson's car when he was arrested. The magazines are entitled *Chicken Hotties, Poultry Porno*, and *Feathers in Leather*. *not hearsay - magazines aren't assertions*

14. To prove that Daniel was incompetent to make a valid will, a neighbor testifies that that on three occasions in December 2008, he saw Daniel outside in below-zero weather wearing no clothes and singing "We're Having a Heat Wave, a Tropical Heat Wave." *not hearsay. truth of Daniel's heatwave statement doesn't matter - not trying to prove heatwave*

15S. To prove that Walter was hurt five miles from downtown Nita City, Ernie Augen offers testimony that a sign right where the worksite was located stated "Downtown Nita City—5 miles." *hearsay - depends on truth of the sign's assertion of 5 miles*

16. To prove that Dave intended to turn left at the approaching intersection [assume relevancy], Betty, driving the car immediately behind Dave's, would testify that as Dave's car approached the intersection, the left-turn signal went on and the brake light went on. *hearsay - assertion through turn signal no assertion through brake light no attempt to communicate*

17. *P v. D* is an action for involuntary commitment. To prove incompetence of D, P offers D's diary [assume authenticated], which includes many odd entries such as this one for last Thursday: "Woke up at 6 and the Martians were here as usual. We played hopscotch till noon and then traveled in their ship and blew up the Parthenon. Ugly building! For dinner we ate concrete and moonbeams. We watched the late news and they were really honked off that there was nothing about the Parthenon job." *not hearsay - not being admitted for the truth of the assertions*

Hearsay: Prior Statement by Witness

Rule 801(d)(1)

In each case, indicate whether the statement is excluded from the definition of hearsay under 801(d)(1).

1S. To prove that Jerry was one of the bank robbers, prosecution calls Tammy Cassiere, who would testify that at a lineup conducted the next day, when asked if she could identify the men who robbed the bank, she pointed at Tom and Jerry. *admissible - 801 (d)(1)(C) - identification - subj to cross-exam*

2. The State's Attorney's Office is investigating political corruption in Nita City. Paul Caprio is called before a grand jury and states, among other things, that on many occasions he delivered bribe money to Mayor Marion Bacca from various underworld characters. In part as a result of this testimony, Mayor Bacca is indicted for violation of the state bribery statute. The prosecution calls Caprio to testify. When asked if he ever delivered bribe money to the mayor, Caprio states that he did not. To prove that Caprio did deliver bribes to the mayor, the prosecution offers Caprio's grand jury testimony. *admissible - 801(d)(1)(A) - inconsistent statement under perjury*

3. Same case except that Caprio died from unrelated causes a week before the trial. The prosecution offers his grand jury testimony. *inadmissible - not available for cross-exam*

4S. In Walter's case against Roads Are Us, Walter calls his brother, Bill Workman, who was on the job that day. He testifies that Walter told him about ten minutes before the accident that he was frightened and would keep a close lookout because he thought the safety setup was inadequate. Assume this testimony is permitted. On cross-examination, defense counsel asks this question: "Isn't it true that you're Walter's brother and would like to see him recover as much money as possible?" On redirect, Bill is asked to relate that the day after the accident he reported to his friend, Fred, that Walter had made such statement. *admissible - 801(d)(1)(B)(i) - used to rebut*

5S. At Walter's worker's compensation hearing (against Tar Is Us), he testified about the accident. Can Walter introduce the transcript of his testimony against Diana? Can Diana introduce it against Walter?

W can't bolster his own testimony
D can introduce against Walter only if inconsistent

Hearsay: An Opposing Party's Statement

Rule 801(d)(2)

In each case, indicate whether the statement is excluded from the definition of hearsay under 801(d)(2).

1S. *United States v. Allen, Brian, and Charlie* is a criminal prosecution for robbery of a federally insured bank and for conspiracy to commit robbery. Assume that the government has already produced evidence of a conspiratorial agreement among the three. The government now seeks to introduce a telephone conversation between Allen and Brian recorded by a wiretap placed on Brian's phone pursuant to a lawful court order. During that conversation, Brian can be heard saying to Allen, "You go ahead and get a floor plan of the bank, I'll get the work schedules of the bank guards, and I've already got Charlie working on getting us the guns from a mail-order house so don't worry about that—we're not going to use the guns registered to us." After authenticating the recording, the government offers this clip of the recording to prove that Allen, Brian, and Charlie each did these things. Brian (the person whose voice is on the recording being offered) objects. *admissible b/c offered by prosecutor - offered by opposing party made by other opposing party*

2. Same case, same offered evidence. Allen and Charlie object. *admissible b/c conspirators 801(d)(2)(E)*

3. *P Inc. v. D Inc.* involves enforcement of a contract for a sale of widgets. D Inc. denies any contract existed. To prove that a contract existed, P Inc. calls W who would testify that a month ago, X, the president of D Inc., said to him: "Boy, I'm in a bind. I made a bad deal with a guy from P Inc. for widgets and now we're getting sued. Thank God the deal wasn't in writing so we can just deny it." *admissible 801(d)(2)(D) or agent or employee - party authorized*

4S. In the prosecution of Tom for possession of a controlled substance, the prosecution offers Tom's confession typed on a laptop after it is authenticated by Rory. *admissible 801(d)(2)(A)*

5S. To prove that Jerry robbed the bank, the prosecution offers Rory's testimony that when he arrested Tom and Jerry, he said to Jerry, "You robbed the bank, didn't you?" and Jerry said nothing, but merely looked down at the ground. *inadmissible if Mirandized*

6S. In Deena's product liability action against National Motors, National Motors calls Perry Notfall (who took Deena to the hospital following the accident), who would testify that Diana said to Perry: "The window just busted onto her. I kept telling her and her brother not to keep punching that window or sooner or later it would get so weak it would bust." Deena objects. *inadmissible under 801(d) b/c not statement by opposing party, statement made by 3rd party*

or

admissible under 801(d)(2)(A) by mother in representative capacity

Hearsay Exceptions

Rule 803(1)–(4)

1S. Walter calls Ernie Augen to testify that immediately after the accident, Walter's brother, Bill, screamed out: "Oh, my God! Walter's got tar all over him. That stupid woman drove right off the road and knocked the vat over."
Present sense impression & excited utterance – admissible

2S. Ernie would testify that he heard Walter say to Bill about thirty seconds after the accident: "Jesus, Bill, it feels like my chest and face are on fire! The pain is tremendous! I knew there was not enough protection at this site."
Present sense impression & excited utterance – admissible

3S. Perry would testify that when the EMS crew arrived, Bill said to Perry Notfall, "My brother says his face and chest feel like they're on fire, and he's in a lot of pain."

4. *P v. D.* To prove that D was jogging in the Meadowdale subdivision on the afternoon of August 12, P calls Sarah Johnson, who lives in Meadowdale. Johnson would testify that on the afternoon of August 12, she was watching television, and her husband, Howard, was looking out the front window and said to her, "There goes that idiot D jogging by. What a moron!"

5. To prove that X was in Germany in the summer of 2013 [assume relevant], Plaintiff offers the testimony of Y that X said to Y in March of 2013, "I'm going to Europe this summer." [Neither X nor Y are parties.]

6. *State v. Dwayne* involves the homicide of Victor Timm twenty years ago. When Timm was killed, his sister, Vickie, then sixteen years old, witnessed the homicide. She got a good look at the killer, but years of efforts by Vickie and the police to find the man produced nothing. Just this past spring, Vickie was attending the Policeman's Ball when a man walked past her table. Vickie's eyes lit up very wide, and she pointed and screamed, "That's the man who killed Vic!" She died several minutes later from a burst aneurysm. The man who walked past the table was Dwayne. At Dwayne's trial, to prove that Vickie identified Dwayne as Vic's killer, State calls Officer Prientenos, who was seated next to Vickie at the table and witnessed the event, to testify about what Vickie said.

National Institute for Trial Advocacy

Hearsay Exceptions

Rule 803(5)–(8)

1S. Walter offers the following entries from an authenticated copy of Rory Croot's police report on the accident on Route 49. Diana and Roads Are Us object to each. How should the court rule?

   a. Rory's measurements of the length of the skid marks Diana's car left on Route 49.

   b. Rory's description of the damage to Diana's car and to the vat.

   c. Rory's verbatim account of the statement of Ernie Augen concerning what Ernie saw when the accident happened.

2S. At Deena's trial against National Motors, Deena offers:

   a. A certified copy of the car's registration showing Donald Driver as registered owner.

   b. A copy from Ned's National Motors Sales of the contract of sale of the car to Donald Driver.

   c. A copy received in discovery from National Motors of the proof of the manufacture of the vehicle by National together with all normal presale inspections.

3. To prove the license number of a car involved in a hit-and-run accident, the prosecution wants to introduce the testimony of Gary Vecchio, who saw the accident, saw the car take off, and immediately wrote down the license number of the car on a sheet of paper so he wouldn't forget it. However, now Gary cannot remember the number, but has the paper on which is written 64A1382.

4. Same as question 3 except that Gary had no paper, but had a camera and took a picture of the fleeing car. Although he cannot remember the license number, he has the photograph in which one can see the retreating car's license plate— 64A1382.

Hearsay Exceptions

Rule 803(9)–(23)

1. *Paul Aintiff v. Doctor Douglas* is a malpractice action for prescribing the wrong pharmaceutical for Paul's illness. To prove that Nexium is in a class of drugs called "proton pump inhibitors," Paul offers to introduce the *Physician's Desk Reference*, which lists Nexium under "Proton Pump Inhibitors."
    803(18)

2. *State v. Randolf* is a criminal prosecution for bigamy. To prove that Randolf was married to Wanda, prosecution introduces a certified copy of the record of a marriage conducted two years ago between Randolf and Wanda.
    803(9)

3S. After Ernie Augen testifies for Walter, counsel for Roads Are Us introduces a six-year-old conviction from another state of Ernie for robbery.
    609 ?   803(22)

4. *P v. D.* Assume it would help P to prove that D attempted to telephone P on October 1. P testifies that on the evening of October 1, he looked at his "ID record" on his phone, a device that shows the phone number of the person currently placing a call and saw the number 219-462-2222. To prove that D was the caller, P introduces a copy of the local telephone directory, which shows that the number assigned to D is 219-462-2222.
    803(17)

5. P calls X, who testifies. D impeaches X with a prior conviction. P now calls CW, who would testify that he knows many people who know X and that X has a reputation for being an honest, truthful person.
    803(21)

HEARSAY EXCEPTIONS

RULE 804(b)(1)–(2)

1. *State v. Douglas* is a criminal prosecution for the aggravated battery of Victor Timm. When Victor was found badly beaten and unconscious on the floor of his convenience store, he was rushed to the hospital. Being a devout Catholic, he requested last rites. A priest was summoned and performed them. Later that evening, about six hours after he had been admitted, Victor said to an attending nurse, Betty, "That darn Douglas hated me for years and finally did me in. I don't think I'll last the night." Victor recovered. However, two days before Douglas' trial, Victor died in a car accident. To prove that Douglas beat Victor, prosecution calls Betty to relate Vic's statements to her.

2. Same as question 1 except that Victor died minutes after making the statement to Betty and the charge against Douglas is homicide. Can the prosecution have Betty relay Victor's statements?

3S. Walter calls Ernie Augen, who testifies to what he saw at the accident. Walter obtains a judgment against Diana, and Diana appeals. The appellate court reverses and remands on an issue wholly unrelated to Ernie's testimony. Ernie moves to the Solomon Islands without letting anyone know. (In fact, you and your classmates are the only ones who do know.) At the retrial, Walter offers the transcript of Ernie's testimony from the first trial.

4. The State's Attorney's Office is investigating political corruption in the Nita City. Paul Caprio is called before a grand jury and states, among other things, that on many occasions he delivered bribe money to Mayor Marion Bacca from various underworld characters. In part as a result of this testimony, Mayor Bacca is indicted for violation of the state bribery statute. Paul dies (by mistakenly drinking rat poison) a week before the trial. The prosecution offers Paul's grand jury testimony to prove the truth of its content.

Hearsay Exceptions

Rule 804(b)(3)–(6)

1. Assume it is relevant that on June 15, 2013, American Steel, Inc., was solvent. Plaintiff, to prove solvency, calls James Vidne, who would testify that on June 20, 2013, Heddy Buckel, CEO of the large auto company, Admiral Motors, stated to James, "Golly, I'm in a mess. I've got to find $5 million in cash-flow somewhere to pay off our debt to American Steel." [Neither Admiral Motors nor Heddy Buckel is a party to this action.]

2S. At Deena's trial against National Motors, Deena takes the stand and is asked whether she is the daughter of Diana. National Motors objects that such is hearsay.

3. The State's Attorney's Office is investigating political corruption in the Nita City. Paul Caprio is called before a grand jury and states, among other things, that on many occasions he delivered bribe money to Mayor Marion Bacca from various underworld characters. In part as a result of this testimony, Mayor Bacca is indicted for violation of the state bribery statute. Caprio dies (by mistakenly drinking rat poison) a week before the trial, and there is some evidence that Bacca put the rat poison in Caprio's drink. The prosecution offers Caprio's grand jury testimony to prove the truth of its content, citing Rule 804(b)(6). How should the court proceed?

Lay Opinion

Rule 701

1S. Walter offers the testimony of his coworker, Connie, that the blue sedan (Diana's car) was "going over forty miles per hour when it swerved off the roadway." Diana objects.

    a. With the proper foundation, is this admissible lay opinion?
        Yes

    b. How would you lay the foundation for this opinion?
        estimate based on 1st hand knowledge, familiarity est. speed

2S. Walter offers Connie's testimony that the blue sedan was "speeding" when it left the roadway. Is this admissible? *yes if "speeding" is "above the limit" rather than "reckless driving"*

3S. In Sam's criminal trial for minor consumption, prosecution offers the testimony of Guy Pieton, who would testify that when Sam was led out in handcuffs, his breath smelled of alcohol, he was staggering, his speech was slurred, and that Guy formed the clear impression that Sam was intoxicated.

    Yes

Expert Testimony

Rules 702–706

1S. Walter calls Hiram Seguro, a construction safety engineer, to testify that the protections for workers that Roads Are Us erected were well below the custom in the industry. Prepare a list of questions to qualify Hiram to testify as an expert on this matter. *school? how long on the job? experience in safety customs?*

"How do you know what you're telling us?"

2S. Does a sufficient body of knowledge on road construction safety exist to warrant the admissibility of Hiram's opinion on such a matter?

3S. Can Hiram be asked if, in his opinion, Roads Are Us was negligent? Can Hiram be asked if, in his opinion, a proper safety setup would have prevented the injury to Walter (in other words, that the actual setup was the cause in fact of the injury)? *No on negligence. → legal term of art Yes on setup.*

4S. Walter calls Chris Corrigan, a mechanical engineer specializing in accident reconstruction. Assume Chris is qualified as an expert. He would, using standard formulas taking into account the strength of materials and other factors, testify that Diana's car struck the vat of tar at thirty-eight miles per hour. Chris, of course, did not see the accident, but was shown Diana's car and the vat several weeks later, identified as such by Rory Croot. May Chris so testify? *Yes · reliable methods - hearsay doesn't bar the testimony - normal reliance*

5S. Before trial, Roads Are Us asks the court to appoint an expert witness to duplicate the tests that Chris performed. Should the court appoint an expert under Rule 706? *No - get your own expert don't make taxpayers pay for the expert*

AUTHENTICATION AND IDENTIFICATION

RULES 901–903

1S. Just before Sam is arrested for underage drinking, Barb, one of the proprietors of the brewpub, receives a phone call. A female voice says: "I'm across the street from you with a cell phone and can see Sam Swill drinking a beer in your place. He's a student of mine at the high school. Are you aware he is only sixteen? Don't let him get you guys in trouble." Discuss the various ways, depending on available evidence, the prosecution can authenticate the call as having come from Vivian Sander.

2S. Sam's counsel objects, after a foundation authenticating the voice as Vivian's is presented, indicating that he plans on calling Vivian Sander, who will deny having made any such call to the brewpub. To what standard must the judge be persuaded that it was Vivian's voice on the call before admitting testimony about the call? *perponderance of the evidence*

3S. Same facts as question 1S except that no one answered the phone and the caller left the same message as voicemail that has been preserved. Discuss the various ways to authenticate the call.

4S. In Tom and Jerry's robbery trial, Tammy Cassiere produces a handwritten note given to her by one of the robbers. Discuss the various ways to authenticate the handwriting as Jerry's.

5S. In Tom's trial for cocaine possession, the prosecution wants to introduce the cocaine that Rory confiscated from Tom. After the arrest, Rory turned the evidence over to Evan "Dense" Lockerby, who placed it in the locked evidence room. It was released once to Timothy Pomoc at the crime laboratory, who tested a portion of it. It tested positive for cocaine. Timothy returned it to Evan at the lockup. Rory brought it to court with him. How can the cocaine be authenticated as that taken from Tom and shown to be cocaine? *everyone in the chain of custody testifies*

The Original Writing ("Best Evidence") Rule

Rules 1001–1008

1S. In Deena's action against National Motors, Deena calls Diana to testify about what Diana told the ambulance driver who took Deena to the emergency room. National Motors objects based on the Original Writing Rule because Diana's verbatim statement is in the ambulance report.
content of report not at issue - what was said is at issue

2S. Deena next calls the ambulance driver to testify from his recollection about what he wrote in the report. National Motors makes the same objection.
content IS at issue b/c he's being asked what he wrote

3S. Assume that Deena wants to introduce the ambulance report. As the result of a flood two months ago, all of the ambulance company's records were destroyed. The hospital to which Deena was taken, however, has a copy of the ambulance report. National Motors objects to the introduction of the copy.
copy is considered "original"

4S. Same as question 3S, except that instead of introducing the copy the hospital has, Deena calls her uncle, Garrett, who, while he did not witness the accident, read the entire hospital record of Deena's visit, including the ambulance report. Deena asks Garrett to state what was in the hospital copy of the ambulance report. National Motors objects.
best evidence rule applies - need the original - recollection not enough

5S. In Walter's case, Diana is called to testify about what was ~~written~~ said on the side of the vat she hit. She would state, if required to, that it said, "Hot Tar." Diana objects based on the Original Writing Rule.

6S. a. In the controlled-substance prosecution of Tom, the prosecution offers through Rory Croot during its case-in-chief a printed confession; Rory would testify that Tom composed this confession on a laptop that Rory let him use in the police station. Tom's attorney states that he will call both Tom and Jerry to testify that at no time during the interrogation did Tom do any such thing, but, instead, made a handwritten statement that denied any criminal involvement. Tom's attorney further states Tom will so testify during the defense case and will present a copy of the handwritten statement that Rory made for Tom on the copy machine at the jail. Should Rory be permitted to testify and introduce the printed confession? [Assume that *Miranda* was complied with.]

   b. During the defense case-in-chief, Tom testifies that he made the handwritten note and the defense introduces it. The prosecution objects and states that no such note was ever given to the police. What should the court do?

REAL AND DEMONSTRATIVE EVIDENCE

1S. Walter offers, after proper authentication, the vat that Diana's car hit and spilled hot tar on Walter. It can be brought in on a dolly, and the indentation where it was hit is still evident. Diana objects.

2S. Walter introduces a photograph of Walter lying on the ground covered with tar near the overturned vat. No one knows who took the photograph. Assuming that Ernie Augen viewed the scene at that time, can the photograph be authenticated by him? How?

3S. Walter introduces each of the following. Assuming they can be properly authenticated and that Diana objects to each using her best argument, which should be admitted and why?

   a. A photograph of Walter's broken watch that the vat slammed into.

   b. Photographs of Walter's face after each of his four skin-graft operations.

   c. A six-hour movie of the third skin-graft operation.

4. *P v. D* is a case alleging the intentional tort of battery in P's apartment. In describing the layout of the apartment, which of the following methods could P employ:

   a. Have P draw a sketch of the apartment while on the stand.

   b. Introduce a floor-plan drawn to scale by an architect.

   c. Introduce a computerized 360-degree authenticated web-camera tour of the apartment.

5S. In the robbery trial of Tom and Jerry, defendants ask that the jury be taken to view the Nickel & Dime Savings Bank. Prosecution objects. What result?

6S. Walter introduces a photograph of State Highway 49 at the point of the construction site. The photograph was taken eighteen months after the accident. Roads Are Us objects.

Social Policy Exclusions

Rules 407–412

1S. In the action against Roads Are Us, to prove that defendant's employee Eddie Jalan was negligent, Walter wants to introduce evidence that a week after the accident, Roads Are Us fired Eddie, who had set up the safety system for the Route 49 project. Roads Are Us objects. *excluded under 407 subsequent remedial measures – want to encourage remediation*

2S. In the same action, to prove the negligence of the safety engineers of Roads Are Us, Walter wants to introduce evidence that a month after the accident, all of its safety engineers were sent to a national conference on Road Construction Safety. *excluded under 407*

3S. Walter calls another coworker, Carmen, who would testify that he was kneeling by Walter waiting for the ambulance when Harry Buckel, CEO of Roads Are Us, arrived on the scene, walked over to Walter, and said: "Buddy, don't worry, Roads Are Us will pay all of your medical bills. The safety system here looks a little thin to me." Roads Are Us objects to introduction of the first sentence. What result? *excluded under 409*

4S. Roads Are Us objects to introduction of the second sentence. What result? *admitted – 409 doesn't exclude, passes 403 balance*

5S. Walter asks Carmen to testify that Diana came over to Walter as he was lying on the ground and said: "Oh, my God! I'm sorry. If you promise not to seek excess coverage from me, I'll admit in court that this was my fault and you can get whatever you can from my liability insurance carrier. I was going way too fast and not paying much attention." Diana objects to this evidence. What result and why? *excluded under 408 – statements in conjunction w/ negotiation*

· quid pro quo
· bargaining

6S. Roads Are Us argues to the jury that the State's decision to keep the road open during construction was negligent (although the State is not a party to the action). Roads Are Us introduces a letter from the State Commissioner for Highway Safety issued three days after the accident that states, in part: "No State Highways shall be kept open during construction on such road without express written pre-approval from this office." Walter objects based on Rule 407. What result? Does it depend on other state law? *excluded under 407 even though it's 3rd party remedial measures? maybe/ maybe not*

7S. In the controlled-substance prosecution of Tom, Rory would testify that after *Miranda* warnings were given and waived, Rory said, "Tom, this whole thing will work out better for you if you just come clean on the coke." At that point, Rory states that Tom asked for a laptop and typed out a confession. Tom objects that introduction would violate Rule 410. What result? *admitted – 410 doesn't apply b/c this isn't a plea deal – attny for pros. must be present*

Character and Habit

Rules 404–406; 413–415

1S. Roads Are Us calls Hans Klug, safety officer for Roads Are Us, to testify that whenever the company has men working construction on roads not closed to the public, the company has a standard policy of placing a flag man 100 yards away from the vat toward approaching traffic with a sign that says, "Slow Down. Men Working." Diana and Walter both object.
  - admissible b/c policy is regularly employed

2S. Prosecution offers testimony of Mr. Thomas Kennari, history teacher and lunchroom supervisor at Sam's high school, stating that on three prior occasions he caught Sam drinking beer at lunch in violation of both state law and school rules. *- inadmissible character evidence/past bad acts not regular enough to be habit*

3S. Prosecution offers the testimony of Frieda Tilhenger, who lives in the apartment over the brewpub. Frieda testifies that on each of the fifteen times she walked home from school (usually she takes the school bus) she walked behind Sam, and that on each occasion he went into the brewpub. *probably excluded under 403*
  - admissible as habit - 15/15 is sufficiently reliable/regular

4. *State v. Donald Duker* for the battery of Victor Timm. Donald calls Woody Vidne to testify. Discuss the admissibility of each of the following:

   a. I have known Victor Timm *[victim]* for many years at church and on several committees for the City. In my opinion, he is a very violent person.
      - admissible to prove that the Δ would have been fearful/acted in self def.

   b. Once I saw Victor hit an elderly lady with a shovel.

   c. I have talked with many persons who know Victor Timm well because they work at the same plant. They all state that he has the reputation of being a violent person.

   d. The night of the incident, I saw Victor an hour earlier walking down the street and punching every street sign hard.

On the cross-examination of Woody Vidne, the prosecution asks him the following questions. Are they appropriate cross-examination?

   e. Are you aware that Victor Timm is chair of the City's volunteer organization, "Conciliation Services," which offers free mediation and conciliation services to all citizens?

f.   Are you aware that Donald Duker beat up a girl scout last year?

On rebuttal, the prosecution calls Tessie Vittna to testify as follows. Is each appropriate?

g.   I have known Donald Duker at work for the past eighteen years, and, in my opinion, he is a very violent person.

h.   Last week, I saw him beat up a girl scout.

i.   I have spoken to many persons in the city who know Victor Timm either at work, at church, or through volunteer work. His reputation for peacefulness and gentleness is legendary in our town.

5.   State next calls Dr. Sy Artz, a practicing psychiatrist, who has had Victor Timm as a patient for ten years. He would testify that based on his extensive knowledge of Victor's psychological makeup, in his opinion, Victor would be incapable of committing any acts of violence.

Impeachment by Prior Inconsistent Statement

Rule 613

[handwritten] * good faith basis needed when the question is an implicit assertion that the witness said something out

Walter calls Ernie Augen, who testifies that he saw Diana's car leave the road, noticed that she was going fast, that she was turned around and appeared to be yelling at the kids in the backseat, and that she crashed into the vat that dumped onto Walter. Ernie is asked why he was walking along Highway 49 at that time and stated that he was going to the store to buy bread. Diana's counsel now proceeds to cross-examine Ernie.

As to each question, address three issues: (a) is the question appropriate cross-examination?; (b) does the question require a good-faith basis?; and (c) given the question and answer, will Diana's lawyer be able to introduce extrinsic evidence on the subject?

1. Q: Mr. Augen, did you ever tell anyone a different story about this incident than what you testified to today? *[handwritten]* a: yes

   A: No. *[handwritten]* b: ~~yes~~ asked in non-accusatory manner, not implicitly asserting
   c:

2. Q: Mr. Augen, isn't it true that the day after the incident, you told Randy Bruit when you met for lunch at the brewpub that the woman driving the car was paying close attention and traveling at a reasonable rate of speed?

   A: I said no such thing. *[handwritten]* a: yes
   b: yes → implicit assertion
   c: yes b/c question relates to a core issue of trial

3. Q: Mr. Augen, isn't it true that later the day of the incident, you told your friend, Frank Copain, that you were walking along Highway 49 to go to the store and buy some soup when you saw the incident?

   A: I don't remember. *[handwritten]* a: yes
   b: yes
   c: no

4. Q: Mr. Augen, isn't it true that you usually wear contacts and were not wearing them that day? *[handwritten]* a: ~~yes~~ no - asking two Q's at once

   A: No, I had them on. *[handwritten]* b: yes
   c: no - b/c no dispute

   Q: Didn't you tell your friend, Frank, that you weren't wearing your contacts?

   A: Yes, I did, but I was mistaken. I remembered later that I had them on.

5. A: Mr. Augen, how far from Walter were you when you saw the tar spill on him?

   A: Between twenty and forty feet.

   a: yes

   b: yes - implied assertion

   c: yes - core to the proceeding

   Q: Isn't it true that you gave a deposition several months ago and that your answer to this same question was "thirty feet"?

   A: I don't know.

IMPEACHMENT BY PRIOR CONVICTION

↳ probative value goes to witness' truthfulness

RULE 609

1S. In Tom's prosecution for possession of cocaine, Tom testifies that he did not possess cocaine, but that Jerry must have planted it on him when he saw Rory Croot coming to arrest them. The prosecution wants to introduce evidence of five prior convictions of Tom. Discuss the admissibility of each:

a. A conviction for battery eighteen years ago for which Tom served three months in prison. *• excluded under 609(b)*
10yr exclusion → released more than 10yrs ago
• probative value doesn't outweigh prejudice

b. A conviction (in federal court) for perjury fourteen years ago for which Tom served two months in prison. *admissible even though older than 10yrs b/c probative value outweigns prejudice*

c. A conviction for arson eleven years ago for which Tom served four years of an eight-year sentence. *excluded by 609(a)(1)(B)*
probative value doesn't outweigh potential prejudice

d. A conviction for possession of cocaine two years ago (a crime punishable by imprisonment for up to eighteen months) for which Tom received probation. *excluded under 609(a)(1)(B)*
probative value doesn't outweigh potential prejudice

e. A conviction four years ago for "theft by deception" for which Tom served nine months in prison. *admissible under 609(a)(2) - crime of deceit comes in regardless of prejudice unless >10yrs old - then apply reversal 403 balancing test*

2S. After Diana testifies in her own defense, Walter's counsel wishes to introduce a conviction of Diana eight years ago for "reckless driving causing a fatality," a crime punishable by up to two years in prison and for which Diana received a three-month home detention. *• per 609(a)(1)(A) - Diana is not a criminal defendant in this case so we apply 403*
• excluded under 403 b/c of unfair prejudice

✱ 609(b) - even if excluded b/c older than 10yrs, must do reverse 403 balancing test

IMPEACHMENT BY PRIOR MISCONDUCT

RULE 608

1S. At Tom's trial for possession of cocaine, Tom testifies in his own defense. On cross-examination, the prosecutor asks for permission to ask each of the following questions: 1) should the court permit the question?; and 2) if Tom denies it, may the prosecutor offer extrinsic evidence? [Assume any necessary good-faith basis.]

a. Isn't it true that you embezzled from your employer last year?

b. Isn't it true that fifteen years ago you were arrested for scamming an old lady out of $2,000?

c. Isn't it true that you went to a party several years ago with Jimmy Joint and you both toked marijuana?

d. Isn't it true that last year you threw a hamster out of a twentieth-story window?

Appellate Review of Evidentiary Rulings

Rule 103

In each case, indicate what standard of review the appellate court should use and the probable outcome.

1S. Winifred, who came upon the scene of Walter's injury an hour after the collision, is asked by Walter's counsel to relate a statement made by Xerxes to Winifred: "You should have seen it! This goofy car ran off the road and knocked equipment over on this poor sap." Xerxes is unavailable. Objection: Hearsay. Judge overrules the objection finding that this is an excited utterance. Diana loses the case and appeals.

2S. Walter wants to offer a writing that his witness, X, claims is a regularly kept business record of Tar Is Us. Diana's witness, Y, claims that it is not a regularly kept record of Tar Is Us. Both X and Y work for Tar Is Us. The judge decides that it is not a regularly kept record and excludes it.

    a. Walter makes no offer of proof, loses, and appeals.

    b. Walter makes an offer of proof, loses, and appeals.

3S. At Jerry's trial for robbery, Jerry takes the stand. On cross-examination, for impeachment only, the prosecutor brings out that Jerry was convicted for robbery twice within the last three years. Jerry is convicted.

    a. Jerry never objected to the evidence as improper impeachment.

    b. Jerry objected, but the judge overruled and allowed it for impeachment.

    c. Jerry did not ask for an instruction limiting the conviction to impeachment, and the judge gave none, thus allowing the jury to use it as character for conformity evidence.

    d. Jerry did ask for such a limiting instruction, and the judge gave none.

4S. At Walter's trial, Walker testifies as an eyewitness for Walter. Over Walter's objection, Diana's counsel is permitted to ask on cross-examination: "Isn't it true that four years ago you slugged a boy on the little-league team you coached because he dropped a fly ball?" [Assume a good-faith basis.]

5. *P v. D.* P wins. After trial, D discovers that P's lawyer and the trial judge had a deal in which the judge gets one-half of the lawyer's share. This was a jury case. D appeals.

6. *U.S. v. D.* Government witness W's credibility is attacked by D. Government puts on E, an expert polygraph examiner, to testify that W passed a polygraph on this testimony. D objects. Judge lets E testify. D loses and appeals.

Judicial Notice

Rule 201

1. May the following be judicially noticed?

   a. The reciprocal of .125 is eight.

   b. When Diana's car left the road and hit the vat, the weather conditions in Nita were seventy-one degrees (Fahrenheit) and sunny.

   c. The roadway immediately near the point of her car's exit was dry and uncluttered with any debris.

   d. John Adams was the second president of the United States.

   e. Elvis Presley was the best singer ever.

   f. Zimbabwe is located on the continent of Africa.

   g. Dave, the defendant in a battery prosecution, has a reputation for violence.

   h. The ingredients in the pharmaceutical Nexium are those listed in the *Physician's Desk Reference* under "Nexium."

2S. In Tom's trial for possession of cocaine, the statute elevates the offense's grade if the value of the possessed cocaine is $1,000 or more. The prosecution's expert has already testified about the weight of the cocaine found on Tom. Tom's counsel asks the court to take judicial notice that the value of such amount is under $1,000. Prosecution objects. How should the court rule?

Privileges

Rules 501–502

1S.   Assume (for purposes of this question only) that Walter brought his action against Diana and Roads Are Us in the federal district court for the District of Nita as a diversity action (assume all necessary diversity requirements are met). Diana calls Walter's doctor, Dr. Hank House, to testify to certain things that Walter said to him about the amount of pain Walter experienced throughout the grafting procedures. Assume that the federal rules make no provision for a doctor-patient privilege but that Nita state law has a statutory provision clearly making all conversations between a doctor and patient privileged. Which law should the court apply?

2S.   In connection with Deena's action against National Motors, Diana takes Deena to an attorney, Allen Avoka, and retains Allen to represent Deena. [Eventually, Allen files an action on Deena's behalf through Diana as guardian ad litem.] In connection with each of the following, indicate whether the conversation is privileged:

   a.   Deena recounts the story of the accident and her subsequent medical treatment in the presence of Diana and Allen.

   b.   Same as question 2Sa, except assume that Diana's friend and next-door neighbor, Sally, is in the room also.

   c.   Same as question 2Sa, except assume that Allen's investigator, Sam Buscador, is present also.

   d.   Same as question 2Sa, except that an escaped mental patient is hiding inside a closet in Allen's office and can hear the conversation, though no one knows he is there.

   e.   Later that week, Allen calls Ernie Augen into his office and interviews him.

   f.   Ernie reports to Allen something that Deena said to him after the accident.

3. Dwayne is being prosecuted for the aggravated battery of Victor Timm. The prosecution wants to introduce each of the following, and Dwayne objects to each based on privilege grounds. Assume that the state law of privilege is the same as federal law.

    a. When Dwayne returned home (roughly thirty minutes after the alleged battery), he said to his wife, Jane, "Boy I just knocked the stuffing out of that jerk Victor Timm."

    b. Jane noticed that when Dwayne got out of his car he had blood on his hands, shirt, and pants.

4S. Laura Anwalt represents Roads Are Us. When preparing for Walter's trial, the following all occur. Indicate which are privileged communications between an attorney and client:

    a. Laura talks with Mary Gestion, Executive Vice President of Roads Are Us, about possible settlement offers and trial strategy.

    b. Laura talks with Frank Capataz, the Roads Are Us foreman at the site, about what he saw at the time of the accident.

    c. Laura asks the company's records custodian to deliver to her all of the logs (which are regularly kept business records) for the two months preceding the incident.

    d. Laura talks to Filbert Flise, who was assigned to flag northbound traffic that day, but who admits to her that he had fallen asleep on a nice patch of grass just off the shoulder of the highway.

SECTION B(1)

HEARSAY REVIEW PROBLEMS

Hearsay Review Questions

Each of the following pairs of questions should take three minutes. To save space and cost, I have omitted the spaces for the answers, except for the first question. Notice that the first part asks if the material is hearsay within the definitions of Rule 801, and the second asks if, assuming it is hearsay, it is admissible over a hearsay objection. *Consider no objection other than hearsay.* If you answer the first part that the statement is not hearsay, you need not address the second part, but may simply answer it "Yes" or "Y" or "T." Remember that either of two things can lead to an "F" or "No" answer to the first question, "Hearsay?" Either it does not meet the definition of 801(a)–(c) because it is not assertive or it is not asked for the truth of the matter asserted, etc., *OR* because, even though it does, it fits a hearsay "exclusion" in 801(d). Be sure to give a brief reason why you answer a question as you do: e.g., "effect on hearer," or "statement of party-opponent," or "excited utterance," etc. And, of course, you can use the rule numbers as shorthand. Please ignore Rule 807, the "residual exception," for purposes of these review questions.[1]

1. *State v. Doug* involves a burglary of a bank and theft from its vault. To prove that Doug committed the crimes, State offers the testimony of Janitor—that the morning after the burglary, Janitor, while cleaning the vault, found a briefcase that had been left in the vault. The briefcase had a tag on it that said "Property of Doug."

    Hearsay? __N__

    _____

    _____

    _____

    Admissible? __Y__

    _____

    _____

    _____

2. *United States v. Doogie* involves a prosecution for racketeering. To prove the truth of the statements in the transcript, the U.S. Attorney offers the transcript of the grand jury testimony of Paul Caprio, who had reported to the grand jury many episodes of Doogie's racketeering. The government has no idea where Caprio is now and has used all due diligence to locate him.

    Y, Y   Former Testimony

3. *P v. D* is a breach-of-contract action. P calls W, who testifies that he saw D's truck pull up to P's loading dock and then saw the truck leave moments later

---

1. This format for hearsay questions first appeared in an exam given by Professor Irving Younger and later used by Professor Michael Graham in his *Courtroom Evidence* textbook.

without unloading any of the shipment. To impeach W, D calls X, who would testify that W told X a day after the incident that he watched D's truck being unloaded at P's dock and that the process took over an hour.

Y, Y post inconsistent statement to impeach

4. *State v. Donald* is a prosecution for attempting to jump bail by fleeing. Police testify that they caught Donald on the morning of April 8 driving away from Valparaiso (where he was supposed to turn himself in). To prove that he was not attempting to flee, Donald calls Jerry, a passenger in the car Donald was driving, to testify that he saw a sign saying "Valparaiso, 10 miles" and a few minutes later saw one saying "Valparaiso, 8 miles" and that immediately thereafter, the police pulled Donald over.

N, Y

5. *State v. Doug* is a criminal prosecution for theft of a laptop from Best Buy. To prove that Doug was the thief, prosecution calls Officer Prientenos, who arrived at the scene at Best Buy moments after the theft and found Paul Blart, the store's security officer, lying on the sidewalk just outside the store bleeding profusely from the head. Prientenos would testify that he asked Blart what happened to him and that Blart said, "Well, I saw that guy Doug try to run off with a laptop without paying and ran after him, but I tripped coming out of the store, and my temple banged hard into a shopping cart that some idiot left outside. It hurts real bad—I don't think I'm going to survive." Blart died later that day from his injury. *Y Y dying declaration - doesn't apply!*
could use present sense impression   not a homicide or civil case
or excited utterance

6. *P v. D.* To prove that it was not raining in the Nita City at 3:00 on October 18, P offers the testimony of famous Nita State Civil Procedure law professor, Priscilla Lehrer, that she looked out her window at 3:00 on that day and saw a fraternity soccer game being played on the field next to the law school, that there were about 400 spectators [this being the championship game], and that no one was using an umbrella. *N, Y*

7. *Ron Rook v. Aristotle Academy* is a suit for wrongful discharge of a contract employee. Academy claims that Rook, who had been hired to teach chess, was totally incompetent and could not play chess at even a rudimentary level. To prove that Rook is a wonderful chess player, Rook calls Renu Anand, local resident and cousin of the current world chess champion, Viswanathan Anand, who would authenticate a letter she received from Viswanathan in which he wrote, "I hope it doesn't ever get out that I lost to this geeky guy Ron Rook who lives near you and teaches at the Aristotle Academy and that I had to pay him $100 because I gave him 100-1 odds." Assume that Viswanathan is now back in his home country, India, and cannot be subpoenaed.

Y. N → no exception fits

8. Same case. To prove that Rook is competent to teach chess, Rook offers a letter received several weeks ago from the National Chess Academy offering him $10,000 to give this year's "Spassky Lecture" at their school [assume the letter is properly authenticated]. *N, Y -circumstantial evidence of*
something other than what
is intended to be communicated

9. *State v. D* involves a homicide of V between 9:00 p.m. and 11:00 p.m. on the night of February 6. To prove that D was not at home during that time, prosecution calls Officer O to testify that he went to D's house at 8:45 that night to serve an old warrant, that D's car was not there nor were any lights on in the house, that no one answered the doorbell, and that O waited until past midnight and then gave up.   N, Y

10. *State v. Davey* involves a robbery of a convenience store. To prove that Davey was the robber, State calls Clark Kassierer, the person on duty on the night in question, to testify that three days later he attended a lineup at the police station and when asked if he could identify the robber, pointed at Davey.   N, Y

11. Same case. To impeach the testimony of Clark Kassierer, during the defense's case-in-chief, Davey calls Bob Plappermaul, who would testify that several days after the lineup he talked to Kassierer's sister, Contase. She told Plappermaul that immediately after Clark left the lineup he told Contase that he was unable to identify anyone in the lineup and never really got a good look at the robber.   hearsay w/in hearsay

12. *P v. D* is a negligence action. To prove damages, P offers the testimony of W, who would state that an hour after the accident, P was screaming and yelling, "I'm in horrible pain."   Y, Y   Then existing condition

13. *United States v. D* involves a bank robbery on Friday the thirteenth. Prosecution has already proved that D drove past the bank on the twelfth; its theory is that D was reconnoitering the scene of the crime. To prove why he drove past the bank on the twelfth, D takes the stand and testifies that he received a call on the twelfth from a friend who has since moved to Brazil and that the friend said, "D, go drive past the bank. It's really weird. Fireworks are shooting out of it."

14. *Paul Malato v. Danny Toubib* is an action for medical malpractice in which it is claimed that Danny's removal of a mole caused unnecessary pain. To prove that Paul has an incredibly low threshold for pain and is a hypochondriac, Danny offers a certified copy of a list of prescription pills for pain and other symptoms dispensed to Paul by Walgreen's pharmacy over the past two years.

15. *Paula Viaggiatore v. Local Commuter Railroad* is an action sounding in negligence for injuries allegedly suffered in a fire in the train car in which Paula was riding just after the train left the Lake Bob station. Her ticket, which indicated she was riding in car 10356, has already been placed into evidence. Paula calls Gil Vecchio, who was standing at the Lake Bob station waiting for a train going in the opposite direction. Gil will testify that he noticed that there was a fire in one of the cars. When asked if he can remember the car number, he says: "No, at my age I forget a lot. But because of that and knowing that this might be important, I pulled out my pocket notebook and wrote down the

number of the car." Paula's lawyer asks him if he has the note, and he says he does. He is then asked to look at the note and then asked, "Do you now have independent recollection of the number?" He says: "Honestly, no. But I'm sure I wrote it down right that day." To prove which car Vecchio saw the fire in, Paula's attorney offers the note, which says "10356."

16. *Pete Hudebnik v. Nita County Orchestra, Inc.* is a suit for damages for wrongful discharge under an employment contract. The five-year contract through 2017 could be terminated unilaterally by Nita County only if Pete's piccolo playing deteriorated to the point that he was "incompetent" to play at the necessary level, and Nita County claims that such was the basis of dismissal. To prove his competence, Pete introduces a letter he received last week offering him $80,000 per year to play piccolo for the Chicago Symphony Orchestra.

17. *Paula v. Doug* is a negligence action for personal injuries arising out of an automobile collision. To prove that Doug was traveling too fast, Paula introduces a certified copy of a police report of the accident in which Officer Rory Croot notes that the "skid marks made by the Green Taurus [Doug's car] were 187 feet in length." Y, Y - public record 803(8)(A)(iii)

18. *State v. D* involves a domestic battery. To prove why officer X went to D's house, prosecution offers the testimony of X, stating that X received a call from D's next-door neighbor, who said: "Quick, get someone out immediately to 123 Green Street [D's home]. Someone's getting the tar beat out of them!" N, Y - not offered to prove the truth of the matter - doesn't matter

19. *Pete v. Don* is an action for negligence arising out of Pete's allegation that Don if caller is lying negligently bumped Pete off a roof they were both working on. To prove damages for pain and suffering, Pete calls Dock, the doctor in the emergency room to which Pete was brought that day, to testify that "when Pete was brought in, he was moaning and complaining about being in great pain." Pete is in court and available to testify.

20. Same case. Assume that after the initial consultation, Dock turned Pete over to Amme, the nurse, to give Pete treatment. Assume further that Amme was deposed by Pete's attorney, that Don's attorney was present and conducted cross-examination, and that Amme testified about all the steps she took and reported on the pain Pete experienced both as a result of the fall and the procedures she administered. A week before trial, Amme died. To prove all the matters contained in her deposition, Pete offers the deposition.

21. Same case. To prove that Don was the cause of Pete's injuries, Pete calls Pomoc, a technician who helped both Dock and Amme. Pomoc testifies that during a time when only he was in the room with Pete, Pete said: "Oh, my God! I'm afraid I'm going to die from this. And to think it was that stupid Don that caused all of this." Y, ~~Y~~ N - 804 req's witness unavailability

22. *Victor Timm v. John Cabosser* is a civil action for the intentional tort of battery. To prove that Cabosser had the intent to batter Victor, Victor offers Tommy Contase, who would testify that he spoke to Cabosser's sister, Sally, a week after the incident, and Sally told Tommy that Cabosser had stated to her that he attacked Victor intentionally.

23. *Arrestee v. Copper* is a tort action for false arrest. To prove that he had probable cause to effectuate the arrest, Copper, a police officer for the Nita City Police Department, offers to testify that he had received a phone call from a local branch of the First National Bank, and the bank president, Rich Guy, told Copper that Rich had just watched Arrestee rob the bank.
    N, Y – not offered for truth – effect on the listener

24. *State v. Dave* involves a robbery. The robber left the bank at 2:17 p.m. on December 10. The bank is on the south side of the Homan River. Dave was arrested at 2:27 p.m. that same day north of the Homan River. The only possible way a person could reach that point from the bank in ten minutes is to cross the Homan Bridge. To prove that he could not have crossed the bridge, Dave calls Oeil, who would testify that from his office window he could see that during the entire afternoon on December 10 there was a sign on the northbound approach to the Homan Bridge that read "Bridge Closed for Repairs." *Y, N – no exception applies*

25. *State v. D* is a criminal action for theft of a coat taken from the coatroom at a restaurant. Assume that the theft statute requires proof that D took the coat knowing it was not his and intending to deprive the owner. The prosecution calls X, who was with D that night. X testifies that D said when he took the coat: "This is a nice one. Some rich guy's just going to have to buy a new one." To impeach X, D calls Y, who would testify that X told Y the day after D took the coat that D said: "I think this is my coat. I certainly hope I'm not making a mistake."

26. *Prima Donna v. Opera House* is a lawsuit for wrongful discharge under a contractual relationship. Opera House notes that the contract gives Opera House the right unilaterally to terminate the contract if Donna's singing deteriorates substantially. To prove that her voice has deteriorated, Opera House offers a picture of the audience during one of her recent recitals. The picture shows that everyone had their hands over their ears and that about ten were vomiting.

27. *P v. D Construction Co.* P was injured when driving his car through a road construction site on I-32 that D had designed. P's car skidded off the narrow lane for northbound traffic. To prove that P was negligent, D offers the testimony of Officer X that at the time of the accident, road signs visible to northbound traffic approaching the site said "Slow Down," "Narrow Lane Ahead," and "Danger, Please Be Careful." *N, Y – not being offered to prove their truth – effect on reader – offered to prove that drivers have notice*

28. Same case. The same testimony is offered to prove that D was not negligent.

29. Same case. During cross-examination of Officer X, P's counsel asks if X ever told anyone else about the signage near the construction site, and X said "No." On rebuttal, to impeach Officer X, P calls Y, who would testify that the day after P's accident X told Y: "I think the contractor on I-32 is in trouble. A car fell off the narrow point at the construction site yesterday, and they had no warning signs."

30. *Seller v. Buyer* is a contract action to collect the price for rutabagas sold by Seller to Buyer during July 2013 under a contract that specified the price to be based on the "national average for rutabagas sold during the month in question." To prove what price should be used to calculate the amount owed, Seller offers a copy of the monthly report on national crop sale averages from the U.S. Department of Agriculture, which states that for July 2013, the national average for "rutabagas was $0.68 per pound."

31. *Pamela v. David's Taxi Company* is a personal injury action for damages Pamela received on Thursday, June 15, 2013, when riding in one of David's taxis driven by Eddie Kutscher. David's fired Eddie on Monday, June 29, 2013. To prove that Eddie was negligent, Pamela offers the testimony of Willa. Willa testified that on Friday, June 16, 2013, Eddie said to Willa, "Wow, yesterday I wasn't paying much attention when driving a fare to the airport and crashed into a tree and she got hurt."

32. Assume that David's lost the case to Pamela and suffered a judgment. David's now sues Eddie for indemnification. To prove Eddie's negligence, David calls Willa to testify to the same statement of Eddie.

33. *State v. Doug* is a criminal prosecution for assault, a crime that requires proof that the defendant, either by conduct or words, threatened another person. To prove Doug committed the crime, the prosecutor offers the testimony of Victor that Doug said to Victor, "I'm going to beat the crap out of you right now!"

34. *P v. D.* To prove that May 8, 2014, was a warm night in Chicago, P calls Vera, the coat-check hostess at the swank Charlie Pacer's Restaurant, to testify that no topcoats were checked that night.

35. *United States v. Drew* involves the violation a federal statute—the Blyer Act[2]— which prohibits anyone convicted of committing a firearm crime from ever selling firearms. Drew was convicted three years ago of a firearm crime. To prove that Drew violated the Blyer Act, the U.S. Attorney calls X to the stand. X would testify that several months ago he talked to Sam about collecting money Sam owed him and Sam said: "OK, I know I owe you, and I plan to

---

2. Fictional. Please do not waste your time trying to find it.

pay you. But first I have to get $500 to pay Drew for a nice gun that he sold me a couple of weeks ago. He was great to trust me for the money, and I want to come through for him."

36. *State v. Duane* involves the battery of Vernon. Duane claims self-defense. To prove that Vernon started the fight, Duane offers the statement of Wally that the day before the incident, Vernon said to Wally: "That Duane guy better watch his back. I'm going to get him one of these days."

37. *P v. D* is an action for personal injury. P calls A, who testifies to what he saw at the accident site. To impeach A, D later introduces an eight-year-old conviction of A for fraud, a crime for which A spent eighteen months in prison.

38. *Prima Ballerina v. Nita Ballet Company.* Prima had signed a ten-year contract with Nita in which Nita paid her $200,000 to dance for them twenty times a year. The Ballet Company has the right to terminate the contract if Prima "substantially loses her dancing talent." In December 2013, the Company terminated Prima under this provision. To prove that she had not substantially lost her talent, Prima offers a letter from the Joffrey Ballet Company offering her $500,000 to appear two nights in July of 2014 in their New York production of *Swan Lake*.

39. In a criminal trial of David for robbery, Timmy Cassiere is called to the stand and asked if he can identify the man who robbed the bank, and he points at David.

40. Plaintiff calls Willa Vidne and asks her, "What is your name?"

41. *State v. Jack Dripper* involves the homicide of Thelma Mimin. Police, responding to calls from a neighbor that screams were coming from Mimin's house, entered to find Thelma dead on the floor from multiple stab wounds. They noticed that an audio recorder was operating in "record" mode. When they replayed the recorder, they heard Thelma reading dialogue for rehearsal purposes from her upcoming play. Suddenly on the tape could be heard the sound of a door being broken in, then a male voice [which has been authenticated as Jack's] saying, "Now you're dead, woman!" followed by a woman's voice [which has been authenticated as Thelma's] saying, "No, Jack, don't," followed by sounds of scuffling and screaming. The prosecution offers to play the tape to prove that Jack killed Thelma.

42. *State v. Cabrera* involves the battery of Victor Timm on Friday night, May 8, in the Nita City. To prove that the defendant, a major league baseball player, was in Baltimore the evening of May 8 (thousands of miles from Nita City), the defense offers a box score from the May 9 *Nita Tribune* from the previous evening's Tigers-Orioles game in Baltimore, including the line, "Cabrera, 4 AB, 2 Runs, 2 Hits, 3 RBIs."

43. Conrad Zumer purchases a Mr. Coffee at Wal-Mart. The unit explodes after one week, and Conrad sues Wal-Mart in warranty. To prove the making of the warranty and its terms, Conrad introduces the written warranty included in the package, including the phrase: "And we promise that this unit will not blow up for at least sixty days."

44. *Bryce Burmer v. Nita State School of Law* involves the wrongful termination of a tenured professor. To prove gross incompetence [a basis for dismissal of tenured professors], Valpachinko introduces a photograph of students in Burmer's Evidence class, 90 percent of whom are sleeping.

45. Same case. To prove competence, Burmer introduces a letter received last month from the Yale Law School offering him a tenured professorship to teach Evidence.

46. *Heirs of Tommy Erblasser v. Devisee of Tommy Erblasser* is a suit seeking to deny probate to a signed will of Tommy proffered by Devisee. To prove that the will was revoked, Heirs offer the testimony of Nancy Amme, a nurse. She testified that Tommy said to her two hours before he died: "I tore up what I think was the last signed copy of that stupid will I made leaving my estate to Devisee. What a jerk he is! I hate his guts. He's cut out. Let my heirs share it."

47. *State v. Dave* involves a robbery of a convenience store. Dave takes the stand and testifies that he was at the house of his friend, Fred, at the time of the alleged robbery on Thursday night. Dave was arrested for the robbery on Friday night. On cross-examination, the prosecution impeaches Dave with a three-year-old conviction for "false informing." To prove the alibi, Dave offers the testimony of Jake that on Friday afternoon, Dave told Jake that he had spent Thursday night at Fred's.

48. Same case. Assume all the testimony in the previous question and assume the court permitted Jake to testify. During the prosecution's case in rebuttal, the State offers the testimony of Renee to impeach Dave. Renee states that on the following Monday, after his release on bail, Dave told Renee that he spent the past Thursday night at the apartment of his girlfriend, Gail.

49. Same case. Assume that Renee is permitted to so testify. To impeach Renee, defense offers a seven-year-old conviction of Renee for aggravated battery, a crime for which Renee spent eighteen months in prison.

50. *United States v. Dean* is a criminal prosecution under a federal bribery statute. To prove bribery, the U.S. Attorney introduces a transcript of the grand jury testimony of Paul Caprio, who testified that he was with Dean when Dean offered Senator Canby Bott $10,000 to vote for a bill. Caprio died two months ago of an unknown cause.

51. *P v. D* is a personal injury action arising out of an automobile collision. To prove damages, P calls X, who would testify that two minutes after the

collision, P was lying on the ground screaming: "Jeeeeeesus this hurts! My leg hurts like hell! Shoot me!"

52. Same case. To prove the length of skid marks left by D's car, P introduces an authenticated copy of the police report in which Officer Rory Croot noted that he measured the skid marks left by D's car and that they were ninety-three feet in length.

53. *Paul v. Doug* is a tort action sounding in intentional battery. Doug pleads self-defense. To prove why Doug was in apprehension of Paul, Doug offers the testimony of Al that the day before the incident, Al told Doug that Bill told Al that Chuck told Bill that Paul was "out to get Doug."

54. *P v. XYZ Lawncare, Inc.*, is an action for property damage alleging that XYZ's employee, E, sprayed P's pet dog with a lawn chemical that killed the dog. P testifies that E said to P, after spraying the lawn: "I think I hit your dog with some spray. Sorry."

55. *P v. D* is a property dispute. W gives favorable testimony for P. On cross-examination, D's counsel attempts to develop W's bias by suggesting that W is an old friend of P's mother. W denies knowing P's mother. Assume there is independent testimony in the case that P's mother's pet nickname for P is "Ducky Lucky." To prove that W knew P's mother, D calls X, who would testify that he often heard W refer to P as "Ducky Lucky."

56. *State v. Dave* involves a burglary of Victor Timm's Music Store. Victor died a month prior to trial. To prove that 100 CDs were stolen in the burglary, State calls police detective Freddie Flic, who would testify as follows: "A week before Vic died, I interviewed him and asked what was stolen. He said he couldn't remember, but that he had made a list immediately after the burglary was discovered and carefully listed what was stolen. He then referred to that list and then remembered what was stolen and told me it was 100 CDs."

57. *P v. D* is a contract claim. D deposes X, who testifies that he observed three carloads of widgets delivered to P's warehouse. P's counsel cross-examines X at the deposition. X is in an automobile accident shortly thereafter and is comatose with little prospect of recovery. To prove that three carloads of widgets were delivered, D offers the deposition.

58. *State v. D* involves an aggravated battery. To prove that D has a peaceful character, D calls W, who would testify that he is familiar with D's reputation and that such reputation is one of peacefulness.

59. *P v. D* involves defamation. P is a famous clothing buyer for Macy's. P alleges that during a public meeting, D called P a "big fat liar." To prove that no defamatory remark was made, D calls X, who would testify that he was present at the meeting and heard D refer to P as a "big hat buyer."

60. *State v. D* involves embezzlement. The State introduces evidence that D, a $25,000-per-year accountant, made a $100,000 deposit to her personal bank account on March 15. During D's case-in-chief, D testifies that her rich uncle, U, had made a $100,000 gift to her at noon on that day. In the State's case in rebuttal, to prove that no such gift was made to D by U, State calls W, who would testify that he spoke to U two days before that day and that U said, "I'm so honked off at my niece, D, that I'll never speak to her again." U is available, but called by neither party.

61. *P v. D* is an automobile negligence case. To prove that D was negligent, P offers a certified copy of the police report of the accident that contains this entry: "I then spoke with D, who admitted that he ran the stop sign and hit P's car."

62. *State v. D* involves the homicide of V at a high-school dance. Mr. Smithers, a high-school teacher and a chaperone at the dance, testified that anyone who left the dance had his or her hand stamped with a stamp that left the inked impression, "I was at the Westwood H.S. Dance." To prove that D was at the scene of the homicide, Officer Prientenos would testify that when he arrested D late that night, D's hand bore the impression, "I was at the Westwood H.S. Dance."

63. *State v. D* involves the aggravated battery of V. To prove motive, State calls W, who would testify, "I told D the day before V was beaten that X had told me that Y had told him that V was carrying on a secret affair with D's wife."

64. *P v. D* is a suit to eject D from Beigeacre. To prove that P owns Beigeacre, P offers a certified copy of a recorded deed for Beigeacre from X, grantor, to P, grantee.

65. *P v. D.* To prove the weather was warm on May 10 in Nita City, P offers the testimony of W that W walked around downtown Nita that day and that most people were wearing shorts and perspiring.

66. *State v. D* involves a bank robbery. State calls T, a bank teller, who identifies D as the robber. To prove D was the robber, prosecution offers T's testimony that T identified D's "mug shot" in a mug book (a book of photographs of many persons).

67. *P v. D* is a suit on a promise. Assume that the promise would be legally enforceable if made in Nita, unenforceable if made outside the state. To prove that the promise was made in another state, P offers the testimony of X. X states that he heard D make the promise and at the same time saw on the huge courthouse directly behind D the engraved inscription, "Brevard County, State of Jefferson."

68. *P v. D* involves the custody of three-year-old Suzie, with each party claiming to be the custodial mother. To prove that P was the custodial mother, P calls E,

an employee at the Department of Children and Family Services, who would testify that Suzie was abducted, then found, and that when introduced into a room containing P, D, and six other women, Suzie immediately ran over to P screaming, "Mommy! Mommy!"

69. *P v. D.* Assume it is relevant whether P owed X money on August 15. To prove that P did not owe X money on that date, P offers the testimony of W that on August 15, W had a conversation with X and that X said: "Boy! I'm back in the money now. Yesterday, P finally paid off a large debt he owed me." A week before trial, X suffered a massive stroke and lost his memory.

70. Police respond to a neighbor's call that he, the neighbor, heard a gunshot at Edna Kropp's house. They arrive, break in, and find Edna dead on the floor. Then Officer Prientenos notices Edna's Myna bird in its cage and says, "Hi, little guy." The myna bird says, "Oh, my God, Dilbert. Put that gun down and don't shoot me." In the homicide trial of Dilbert, the prosecution offers Officer Prientenos's testimony about what the Myna bird said.

71. *State v. D* is a criminal prosecution for aggravated battery of V, a clerk in a convenience store. To prove that D battered V, prosecution offers an authenticated video from the store's security camera containing footage of D beating V with a baseball bat.

72. *State v. D* involves the theft of V's car, a 1967 red Corvette. To prove that D was the thief, prosecution offers the testimony of W. W testifies that she spoke to D's sister, S, three days after the theft, and that S said that D had admitted to her the night before that he had recently stolen a Corvette.

73. *P v. D*, a claim for breach of contract. X gives testimony favorable to P. On cross-examination, D's attorney asks X if she is in love with P. X says, "No, I hardly know P." To prove that X is biased in favor of P, D calls Y, who would testify that six months ago X said to Y, "I am deeply in love with P."

74. *Citizen v. Police Officer* is a tort action for false arrest. To prove that Police Officer acted with probable cause, Police Officer's attorney calls Police Officer to testify that "X told me several minutes before the arrest that X had just seen Citizen steal a bicycle."

75. American Steel Company (ASC) includes the following as a standard clause in all of its contracts for the sale of steel:

> **First-time Buyer Discount.** ASC promises to rebate to Buyer 30 percent of the total sale price if sale is over 500 tons and this is the first purchase of 500+ tons of steel ever made by the buyer from ASC or from any other steel producer.

Steel Fabricators Inc. (SFI) signs a contract for 750 tons of steel from ASC, pays the sales price, and now demands a discount under this clause. When

ASC refuses, SFI sues. To prove that SFI is not a first-time buyer of 500+ tons, ASC offers an authenticated written contract for the sale of 510 tons of steel by SFI from the now defunct Columbia Steel Company. That contract is dated November 10, 1957.

76. *P v. D* involves the intentional tort of battery. D claims self-defense and to prove that he was in fear of P, offers the testimony of W that two days before the confrontation, W told D that P was "out to get you."

77. *Passenger v. Bus Co., Inc.,* is a tort suit alleging negligence of Bus Co.'s employee, Driver, leading to Passenger's injuries when the bus hit a utility pole. To prove Driver was negligent, Passenger offers a certified copy of the police report, which states in part: "I talked to Driver, and he admitted to having a four-martini lunch an hour before the incident."

78. *United States v. Donald* is a criminal prosecution for "Impersonating a Federal Officer." To prove Donald committed the crime, U.S. Attorney calls X, who would testify, "Three friends of mine and I were at the Nita Dunes on the beach one night, and Donald approached us wearing a uniform with a patch saying 'U.S. Park Ranger' and said to us, 'I'm confiscating your case of beer in the name of the United States of America,' whereupon he took our beer and left."

79. *United States v. Dave* involves the interstate transportation of a stolen car (Dyer Act). U.S. Attorney calls W and asks if W was with Dave when Dave stole an automobile in Nita and drove it into the State of Jefferson. "No," replies W. To prove that Dave stole and transported the car, U.S. Attorney offers the transcript of W's grand jury testimony, which discloses that W testified: "I was with Dave when he stole the car in Nita and drove it into Jefferson."

80. *Penny v. Dolores* is an action for injuries arising out of an automobile collision. Penny calls Wally, who was standing at the intersection at the time of the collision, and asks him if he saw color of the light governing Penny's car when Penny entered the intersection. "Yes," testifies Wally. "What color was it?" asks Penny's lawyer. "Red," says Wally. To prove that the light was green, Penny calls Investigator, a private detective who works for Penny's lawyer, to testify that he interviewed Wally two days after the accident and Wally told Investigator that the light governing Penny was green.

81. *Professor Phil Ossifer v. Northeast South Nita State at Westfield University* involves the improper discharge of a tenured professor. To counter the University's claim that he neglected his teaching duties, Phil offers an extensive 400-page syllabus for his course, "Epistemology 605: The Meaning of Meaning What is Meant."

82. *Paul v. Dieter* is a civil action for the intentional tort of battery. To prove that Dieter hit Paul, Paul introduces an article from *The Gossiper*, a local newspaper,

dated the day after the incident and containing this sentence: "When asked what happened, Dieter said, 'I beat the tar out of that damn Paul, that's what happened!'"

83. *P v. D* is an action to quiet title to real estate. P calls W, who testifies that P has lived on the property since 1959. To impeach W, D calls X, who would testify that a year ago W told X that P didn't move onto the property until 2008.

84. *United States v. Cadenza* is a federal criminal prosecution for narcotics trafficking. On June 1, Chad Avver walked into the local FBI office and stated that he had on many occasions, as Cadenza's butler, witnessed Cadenza engaging in narcotics trafficking. He now wanted to leave Cadenza's employ and leave town, but he was scared and wanted to be in the witness protection program in exchange for his testimony against Cadenza. The FBI agreed and took a long statement from Chad. Two weeks before the trial date, Chad was found murdered. The U.S. Attorney introduces witnesses who testify that Cadenza ordered the death of Chad. The U.S. District Judge finds as follows: "I find from this testimony that there is a strong probability that Cadenza ordered Chad's death. Indeed, I am persuaded by a preponderance that this is so, but I am not persuaded beyond a reasonable doubt." To prove that Cadenza engaged in narcotics trafficking, U.S. Attorney introduces the statement Chad gave the FBI on June 1.

85. Police arrest X and Y for robbery and conspiracy to rob. They are separated for interrogation purposes, and X makes a voluntary, Mirandized, written statement as follows: "Y and I agreed to rob the bank, and we did rob the bank." At Y's trial, the State calls a police officer, who authenticates X's confession. To prove that Y conspired to rob and robbed, the State offers the written confession of X.

86. *P v. D* involves a breach of a contract entered into on December 31, 2013. D defends on the grounds that the contract is unenforceable because he was under eighteen years of age when he entered the contract. [Assume that eighteen is the legal age for contracting.] To prove that D was over eighteen at the time, P offers a W-4 form that D submitted to his employer stating his date of birth as "July 6, 1995."

87. *P v. D* is an automobile accident case. Assume it is relevant to prove that D turned left off of Main Street onto First Avenue. To prove that D turned left, P calls X, who would testify that he was behind D's car at the intersection of Main and First. X states that D's car had its left turn signal on, but that X looked away at a "young lady in a tank top" and became so transfixed that he never did see which way the car went once the light turned green.

88. *Heirs at Law v. Devisees* is a suit attempting to invalidate a will on the ground that the testator was incompetent. Heirs call W, who would testify that the

day before testator signed the will, W saw testator wandering naked (except for a pair of black socks) through a busy downtown area saying to everyone he encountered, "I don't care what people say; rock and roll is here to stay!"

89. *State v. Dubos* involves a bank robbery. The bank teller testifies that the masked robber "must have recognized my accent, because he started talking to me in Slovak, my native language." To prove that Dubos speaks Slovak, police officer Muldoon would testify that a search of Dubos' house produced twenty books written in Slovak.

90. *State v. Dave* is a prosecution for the burglary of a local store on December 10. To help establish an alibi, the defense calls Wally, a coworker of Dave's in a local office, to testify that on December 6, Wally read an e-mail message from Dave to the entire office, which said, "Have fun in the cold, suckers! I'm leaving tomorrow for a week in Hawaii. Dave."

91. *State v. D* is a prosecution for aggravated battery of V. To prove that D committed the crime, the State offers the testimony of W that five minutes after the attack, he saw D running fast away from the crime scene.

92. *P v. D Pharmaceutical Co.* To prove that its drug, Fantax, was approved by the federal Food and Drug Administration (FDA), D Pharmaceutical offers a copy of the 2012 Official Book of Approved Drugs, a 2,000-page book published by the FDA, which lists Fantax as approved on page 642.

93. *P v. D* is a contract claim. P calls W, who gives testimony favorable to P. During D's case and solely to impeach W, D offers a six-year-old conviction of W for robbery.

94. *Patient v. Doctor* is an action for medical malpractice. Doctor calls Expert, who testifies that it is medically reasonable to prescribe the drug Syntax to a patient already taking daily doses of Flatuquit. During cross-examination, Patient's lawyer asks Expert if the book *Darby on Drug Combinations* is authoritative in the area, and Expert says: "It is the Bible of drug combinations. Dr. Darby is a genius." To prove malpractice, Patient's lawyer seeks to introduce the following sentence from page 862 in the Darby book: "Syntax must never, under any circumstances, be given with any anti-flatulent, including Flatuquit, Fartnot, or Tootaway."

95. *Buyer v. Seller* involves the breach of an alleged contract for the sale of a lawnmower. Buyer alleges the contract was made on Monday. To prove that a contract existed, Buyer calls William, who would testify that he was present with Buyer and Seller on Tuesday and that Seller said to Buyer: "Remember that contract we made yesterday for you to buy my lawnmower for $500? I hope you're not planning to welsh on that deal."

96. *P v. D* is a negligence case. To prove that a particular neighborhood is a residential area, D offers the testimony of W that W saw many children playing in the street there.

97. *P v. D* is a civil action for negligence in connection with an intersection collision. P introduces the police report to show the length of skid marks left by D's car.

98. The U.S. Attorney presents a mail fraud case to a federal grand jury. W testifies that he observed D placing fraudulent materials into the mail. D is indicted. At D's trial, the government calls W and asks him if he ever saw D place fraudulent material in the mail. W says, "No, I never did." To prove that D placed fraudulent material in the mail, the U.S. Attorney introduces a transcript of W's grand jury testimony.

99. *P v. D Corp.* involves damages arising out of an accident P had with E, a truck driver for D Corp. To prove negligence, P offers the testimony of W, who overhead E saying to his boss later that day: "Well, this one idiot who was standing by the side of the road just started screaming immediately after the collision, 'Wow! Did you all see that! The truck was going a million miles an hour and blew through the stop sign!'"

100. *State v. D* involves the battery of V. To prove that D did not like V, the prosecution calls W, who would testify that he (W) saw D give V the finger the day before the alleged battery.

101. *United States v. Donald* is a criminal prosecution for impersonating a federal officer. To prove the actus reus of the crime, the government calls W, who would testify that he saw Donald walk up to X, show an ID badge, and say, "Hey, bud, I'm an agent with the IRS, and I'd like about five minutes of your time."

102. *Long-Lost Heir v. Known Heirs* involves a share of the intestate estate of Wanda, whose husband, Hank, died several years ago. To prove relationship, Long-Lost offers a 1940 entry in the records of the Second Methodist Church showing Long-Lost as having been born to Hank and Wanda.

103. *United States v. Dan* involves bankruptcy fraud, alleging that Dan listed debts in his petition that did not exist. Dan listed that he owed $500,000 to Loanguy for years. To prove that no such debt existed, Government offers the testimony of IRS Agent X, who would testify that he talked with Loanguy a week before Loanguy's death and asked him how much Dan owed him, and Loanguy said: "Nothing. He never owed me any money."

104. *Paul v. D Corp.* To prove that Paul had notice of an 8:00 p.m. meeting on November 15, D Corp. introduces the testimony of W that at 7:00 p.m. on that evening he (W) called Paul's house, that Paul's wife, Paula, answered the phone, and, when W asked Paula where Paul was, Paula said, "He left a few minutes ago and said he was headed to the D Corp. meeting."

105. *Frieda Fashion v. Danny's Dry-Cleaning, Inc.,* is an action claiming damages for clothing that Danny's allegedly ruined. To prove that the damage occurred at Danny's, Frieda calls Curt Estafette, who drove for Danny (who offered a

pick-up and delivery option), but who has since left Danny's and works in construction. Curt would testify that when he was bagging loads for delivery that morning, he noticed that many clothes for different customers had an oily substance that was staining them. He asked the laundress (who retired about two months after this incident) what was going on, and she said: "Oh my, we had a bad leak in one of the machines, and it got this gunk on a lot of stuff. We couldn't get it off with anything."

106. *State v. Douglas* involves a robbery of a gas station. A grainy photograph taken from a security camera at the gas station is run in the local paper with a request for anyone who recognizes the man to contact police. Chris Sonderling calls the police station, identifies himself to Desk Sergeant Dave, and says: "The photo looks like my next-door neighbor Douglas. He has a jacket just like that. And besides, I remember that he was not home that night, and he's almost always home on a Tuesday." Prosecution calls Desk Sergeant Dave to relate the conversation to prove that Douglas was the robber.

107. *P v. D* is a tort action. P calls W, who testifies that the light governing D's direction was red when D drove into the intersection. For the sole purpose of impeaching W, D calls X, who would testify that the day after the accident, W said to X: "I saw an intersectional accident yesterday. It was probably inevitable at that corner because none of the traffic lights in any direction were working."

108. *P v. D.* To prove that it is more than an hour's drive from Nita City to Anchorage, Alaska, P offers the testimony of W that W has seen a sign on I-66 in Nita that says, "Anchorage, Alaska, 3,068 miles."

109. *Paul v. David* is an action for conversion of a steer. To prove that the steer belongs to Paul, Paul offers a picture of the steer that clearly shows the steer is branded with the words "A Steer from Paul's Really Cool Ranch." [PETA is considering a lawsuit against Paul.]

110. Sammy and Sarah Gatte are married. Sarah has a lover, Pezzo. Testimony by a neighbor has already established that whenever Sammy and Sarah are both home, the light in the room on the second floor furthest to the west is off, but that as soon as Sammy leaves, often the light goes on. Further, Pezzo often drives by, but he will only stop and go in the house if that light is on. On a night when independent testimony has established that Sarah was home, to prove that Sammy was not home, Pete Walker would testify that he walked past the house and noticed that the light in that particular room was on.

111. *State v. Dave* involves the theft of Joe's horse, Horsey. To prove Dave was the thief, prosecution offers the testimony of Auctioneer, stating that when he auctioned off Horsey three months before the alleged theft, Dave held up his hand and entered bids at three prices, but was finally outbid by Joe.

112. *P v. D* is a civil action. P's damages include the fact that he will have pain in his leg from the accident for the rest of his life. To help the jury assess damages, P offers a commercially available life-expectancy table that shows that a man P's age has an average additional life expectancy of thirty-eight years.

113. Testimony has already been presented that whenever Homer Inhaber is home, he puts his spare front-door key inside, but whenever he leaves, he puts it in the flower pot hanging by the front door (in case he loses his main one). To prove that Inhaber was not home at a particular time, the neighbor testifies that at that precise time, he looked inside the flower pot and saw the spare key.

114. *State v. Doug* involves driving under the influence of alcohol. To prove intoxication, the State offers a copy of a receipt (which was found in Doug's car when the police found the car smashed against a tree) headed "Alice's Restaurant," showing the same day's date and containing the words, "6 Manhattan Cocktails @ $4.50=$27.00."

115. *Paula v. Debbie* is an action damages arising out of an automobile collision. To prove that Debbie ran the stop sign, Paula offers a copy of the police report signed by Officer Rory Croot that contains the following notation: "Driver of Car 2 [identified earlier in the report as Debbie's car] states that she never saw the stop sign and didn't stop."

116. *Phil v. Dawn* involves an automobile collision case. Phil has testified that the collision rendered him unconscious immediately and for over eight hours. To prove that Phil was conscious soon after the accident, Dawn calls Walter, who would testify that Ralph walked over to Phil's car moments after the collision, put his head inside for about ten seconds, then walked over to Walter and said, "The driver [Phil] just said to me, 'Wow! My leg hurts something fierce!'"

117. Jack and Jackie Jackson, a married African-American couple, sue Ronny, their real estate agent, under an anti-discrimination law, alleging that he refused to show them houses because of their minority status. To prove lack of intent to discriminate because of race, Ronny takes the stand and testifies that he received phone calls from two local bank presidents warning him that the Jacksons had defaulted on three previous home mortgages.

118. *Sigmund Eega v. Sasha Eega* is an action for divorce and property division. [Assume that in Nita, adultery has an effect on property division.] To prove adultery by Sasha, Sigmund testifies that he overheard a conversation between two men at a bar in which each mentioned and laughed about the "Da Bears" tattoo on Sasha Eega's right buttock. Sasha has already testified that no one but her husband, Sigmund, had ever seen the tattoo (except for the tattoo artist, who, upon finishing Sasha's tattoo, was immediately deported by the INS back to his home in Stanstanistan).

119. *Pete v. Dan* involves an allegation that Dan's truck ran a red light and hit Pete's car in the intersection. The accident was four years ago. Pete calls Sheila, who was in the vehicle behind Pete's, and she testifies that Pete had the green light when he entered the intersection. On cross-examination of Sheila, the following occurs:

> Q: Isn't it a fact that you and Pete are engaged to be married?
>
> A: Yes.
>
> Q: When did you start dating?
>
> A: We met two years ago at a party and started dating. It was only after we dated for a few months that we discovered that I had witnessed his accident."

Pete next calls Sheila's mother to testify that the day after the accident, Sheila told her, "Mom, I saw this awful accident yesterday when a truck ran a traffic light and hit some guy right in front of me." This testimony is offered to prove that the truck had the red light and Pete had the green light.

120. *Heirs v. Devisees* is a suit to invalidate a will. To prove the will, which names testator's son, Sonny, as executor and trustee, heirs call Warren, who would testify that two days before the date of the will, the testator said to Warren: "Of all my children, Sonny is the biggest doofus. I wouldn't trust him to get change for a dollar."

121. *State v. Roué* involves theft by deception, alleging that Roué sold cheap watches, claiming that they were Rolexes. State calls Victor Timm who would testify that Roué said to Victor that the watch Roué offered to sell Victor was a Rolex. [There are two answers to this. Which is the best academic answer? Which is the best argument in court?]

122. *Guy Lastimado v. Truckers, Inc. and Dan Guidatore* is a tort action arising out of an accident in which Dan Guidatore, a truck driver for Truckers, Inc., collided with Guy Lastimado's car. The suit alleges both primary negligence by Truckers, Inc., and vicarious liability of Truckers, Inc.. for the negligence of its employee, Dan Guidatore. The day after the accident, Truckers, Inc., fired Guidatore. Lastimado calls James Vidne, who would testify that a week after the accident, Dan Guidatore told James: "Truckers, Inc., never maintained the trucks properly. Every truck was a mess—steering wouldn't work, brakes seldom worked. I didn't do a damn thing wrong. I couldn't help it given the crap I was given to drive. And then *they* fire *me*! Can you believe it?" Truckers, Inc. objects to the introduction of this statement against it.

123. Same as last case, except that the text of Dan Guidatore's statement to James is: "Truckers, Inc., was right to fire me. I entirely spaced out and was paying no

attention when I plowed into Guy Lastimado." Dan Guidatore objects to the statement being admitted against him. Truckers, Inc., objects to the statement being introduced against it.

124. *Singing Star v. Musical Productions, Inc.* (MPI), is a breach of contract. MPI argues that Singing Star's voice is failing badly and that the contract provides that MPI can terminate the five-year deal if the quality of Singing Star's voice "dramatically diminishes." To prove that such has not happened, Singing Star introduces a recent article by the renowned music editor of the *Nita Daily News*, Carmen Vitter, which states that "Singing Star's voice is better than ever, a music-lover's delight."

125. *Patty v. Deloris* is a civil action for the intentional tort of battery. To prove both damages and how the battery took place, Patty calls Wanda. Wanda would testify that she walked over to Patty several minutes after the incident and asked, "What happened, Patty?" and that Patty replied: "That witch clubbed me with a baseball bat for no reason. She was laughing as she did it. My head is throbbing something awful."

126. *P v. D.* To prove that G is X's grandmother, P offers the testimony of X that "G is my grandmother."

127. To prove that X had heard of the movie, *Slumdog Millionaire*, W would testify that he heard X say, "I saw *Slumdog Millionaire* yesterday."

128. To prove that X had seen the movie, *Slumdog Millionaire*, W would testify that he heard X say, "I saw *Slumdog Millionaire* yesterday."

129. To prove that Tom Erblasser lacked testamentary capacity in August 2013, W testified that on several occasions in August 2013 Tom said to W, "I'm Hillary Clinton!"

130. *P v. D* involves the intentional tort of assault. To prove how the assault took place, P offers a motion picture of P and X reenacting the incident.

131. *Pete Malato v. Doogie Toubib* is a malpractice action for a badly botched ear reconstruction. To prove damages, Pete offers the testimony of Wendy, who works with Pete, that since the procedure many of Pete's less sensitive cowork-ers call him "Dumbo."

132. *Agnes Scrittore v. Anne Fringer* is a conversion action for theft of Agnes's manu-script for a short story. Agnes offers the testimony of Rory Croot, who testifies that when he arrested Anne for an unrelated matter, his search incident to arrest turned up a manuscript (which can be authenticated as Agnes's).

133. *P v. D* involves the damage to a coffee mug that was knocked off P's desk by someone at work. Later that day in the break room, P said, "Who broke my nice mug?" A said, "I saw D knock it off your desk when he walked by and it

busted." D, also in the break room, said nothing, but looked down and covered his face with his hands and cried. W, who was also in the break room, is presented to testify to all of the statements made in the break room.

134. *Golf Tournament, Inc. (GTI) v. Sports Promotion, Inc. (SPI)* claims a breach of contract and specifies that SPI had promised that nationally known golfer Puma Forest would appear at GTI's tournament at Boulder Beach, but he did not. To prove that Puma did in fact participate, SPI offers the testimony of Bagger Vance, a laborer at Boulder Beach. Bagger testifies that he loaded all of the pro's bags on the truck to the practice area and that on one of the bags in large orange letters was the writing, "Puma Forest, PGA Professional."

135. *Heirs of Guy Tote v. Sports Arena, Inc.* is a civil wrongful-death action based on premises liability. To prove negligence and the cause of death, the plaintiffs call Parry Notfall, who would testify that a young woman [who cannot now be identified or located] who helped carry Tote to the ambulance, said to Parry: "Please help this guy! He's dying! Oh, my God! He told me that when he stepped on an electric cable on the floor inside he felt electricity shooting through his body and heard his teeth humming!"

136. *P v. D* involves an auto collision. To prove damages, P calls W, who would testify that after the collision, W saw P emerge from his car and limp across the street holding his knee.

137. *P v. D.* To prove P (who lives in Seattle, Washington) was in the Nita City area on May 6, D offers a certified copy of a car rental agreement from Enterprise Rental in Nita that shows that P rented a car from them in Nita on May 2 and returned it to the same site on May 9.

138. *State v. J* involves the battery of A. J claims self-defense. To prove that J was in fear of A, J offers the testimony of I, who would testify as follows: "Ten of us were playing a party game called 'telephone' in which one person communicates a message through the 'telephone' of all intervening party guests who are sitting or standing in a line. A started this particular message by whispering something to B, then B whispered it to C, and so on. I was next to last in the line, and J was last, so this was, under the rules of the game, A's message to J. [Note they are in alphabetical order—isn't that convenient?] After G whispered something to H, H whispered to me, "I'm going to kill you!' And then I whispered the same to J."

139. *P v. D* is a tort action. P deposes W, who says, "The traffic light was green when P went through it." At trial, P calls W and asks him what color the light was when P went through it. W says, "Red." To prove that the light was green, P offers the "green" statement from W's deposition.

140. *State v. Dean* is a prosecution for going eastbound in the westbound lanes of the Nita Toll Road at 4:15 on Sunday afternoon, October 15. D claims that he

was indeed in the westbound lanes, but was, in fact, going west. To prove that D was headed east, State offers, through Officer Prientenos (who confiscated it from D when he arrested him), a ticket stub from a pro football game of the same date, a game that started at noon and ended at about 3:30 in a city about twenty miles west of this point on the Nita Toll Road.

141. *State v. Lefty Louie* involves the burglary of Sam's Appliances and the theft of stoves therefrom. Police officer Sam Buscador would testify that when he was investigating at Sam's, a young boy around eight years old, said to Buscador: "I can help you. A guy who said his name was Lefty Louie told me an hour ago that he stole the stuff and stored it in his warehouse space at Warehouses 'R Us." Buscador obtained a warrant to search Lefty Louie's warehouse space and found the stolen stoves inside. The little boy cannot be located. Can Buscador testify about what the boy told him to show that the warrant was based on probable cause?

142. Same case. Can Buscador testify about what the boy told him to show that Lefty was the thief?

143. *P v. D.* To prove that X graduated high school in 2003 (assume relevance), P offers the testimony of W, who would state that when he asked X in May 2013 when X graduated from high school, X said, "You're a smart guy, so you can figure this out. This summer, I plan to go to my tenth high school reunion."

144. To prove that X (not a party to the action) believed during the afternoon of June 15 that there was a corporate meeting that night, W's testimony that X said to W that afternoon: "I can't play poker tonight. I have to go to a stupid corporate meeting tonight." [This question produces much debate among Evidence scholars.]

145. *Pauly v. Dandy Mowers, Inc.* is a products liability action alleging that the F-85 lawnmower is in a "defective condition, unreasonably dangerous." To prove defectiveness, Pauly offers a letter written by Eddie, an employee in the product-testing division of Dandy Mowers, to his cousin Teddy that says: "These F-85s are blowing up every day in here. The ones that don't blow up throw blades out at about 400 miles per hour. Remember Stretch, who played basketball with us last year? The big guy—six foot six, maybe? He's now five foot ten and answers to the name 'Stumpy.' Nobody wants to work on the F-85 project—it's too damned dangerous!"

146. *Packy v. Doodles* is a negligence case arising out of an automobile collision. To prove contributory negligence, Doodles introduces a properly authenticated newspaper story about the incident that includes this passage: "When asked what caused the accident, Packy said, 'If I hadn't been so distracted talking on my cell phone, I would have been able to stop and avoid this whole thing.'"

147. *P v. D.* To prove that X (a city councilman who is not a party to this action) voted for a city resolution, testimony of W is offered, stating that he was present when the resolution was put before the city council and that when X's name was called during a roll-call vote, X said, "Aye."

148. *State v. D* is a criminal action alleging that D battered V, who was participating in a pro-choice rally. The prosecution asserts that D battered V (among others) because D hates their political views [assume that such would bring the case under a hate-crime provision and enhance the penalty]. D takes the stand and states that he is pro-choice himself. To prove D's political views on this matter, prosecution offers the testimony of Officer O, stating that when he arrested D, D was driving a car with a bumper sticker reading, "BAN ALL ABORTIONS NOW!"

149. *State v. Dieter* is a proceeding for involuntary commitment, alleging that Dieter is incompetent and dangerous. To prove incompetence, State calls Wally, who would testify that Dieter's wife, Marlise, told Wally, "Dieter walks around all the time with a huge butcher knife swiping at people and claiming to be Volkar, son of Conan the Barbarian."

150. *P v. D* involves an intersection collision. P offers a witness who would testify that the sign facing the traffic in the direction D was coming from says, "Stop," and a sign under it says, "Cross traffic does not have to stop."

Section B(2)

Multiple Choice Questions

1. D and X are in an automobile owned by and registered to D. The car strikes P, a pedestrian, who is seriously injured. When the police arrive, both D and X are unconscious on the roadway and taken to the hospital. D dies an hour later. Three days later, X comes out of his coma and asks to see his personal attorney, Larry Anwalt, who he has under retainer. After paying Larry for the consultation, X says, "I want you to know that I was driving the car when it hit that guy." X died two days later. P sues the estate of D for negligence. D's attorney, Carrie Avoka, has a suspicion that D may not have been driving. She learns from her friend, Nancy Amme, that Larry Anwalt visited X in the hospital. Carrie calls Larry to the stand and asks him what, if anything, X told him about the accident. Larry asserts the attorney-client privilege. Carrie asks the court to require Larry to answer the question. The court should:

   A. Compel Larry to testify because any privilege ended with X's death.

   B. Compel Larry to testify because his conversation with X was not privileged.

   C. Determine whether Nita follows the "control group" test or the "subject matter" test, because under each test, the issue would be answered differently.

   D. Permit Larry to invoke the privilege.

2. Consider the following three propositions:

   i. An expert can never give an opinion without first stating the facts on which such opinion is based.

   ii. A person who refuses to promise to tell the truth can never be a witness.

   iii. A duplicate is easier to introduce under the "American rule" than under the "English rule."

   Which, if any, of these propositions are true?

   A. None of them.

   B. i, but not ii or iii.

   C. ii, but not i or iii.

   D. iii, but not i or ii.

   E. i and ii, but not iii.

   F. i and iii, but not ii.

   G. ii and iii, but not i.

   H. All of them.

3. Consider the following preliminary statements:

    i.   A finding that a piece of evidence does not violate the rule on character evidence preliminary to its being introduced.

    ii. A finding that a piece of evidence is not hearsay preliminary to its being introduced.

    iii. A finding that W has personal knowledge of an event preliminary to his testifying about that event.

    On which must the judge be persuaded of the preliminary fact by a "preponderance of the evidence"?

    A. None of them.

    B. i, but not ii or iii.

    C. ii, but not i or iii.

    D. iii, but not i or ii.

    E. i and ii, but not iii.

    F. i and iii, but not ii.

    G. ii and iii, but not i.

    H. All of them.

4. Proponent introduces paragraph one of a letter written by T and sent to both Proponent and Opponent (T is a third person who is not a party to the action). Paragraph one is relevant, and there is no sustainable objection to it (assume it fits an exception to the hearsay rule). Opponent now asks the Court to require Proponent to introduce paragraph two of the same letter on the grounds that it, in fairness, ought to be considered together with paragraph one. Paragraph two, however, unlike paragraph one, consists entirely of statements that are inadmissible character evidence. Proponent objects. The court should:

    A. Require the Proponent to introduce paragraph two if it modifies, explains, or otherwise casts light on paragraph one.

    B. Require the Proponent to introduce paragraph two because his introduction of paragraph one operates as a waiver of the character objection.

    C. Not require the Proponent to introduce paragraph two because as it is Proponent's case, he and he alone can choose what evidence is introduced at this time.

D. Not require the Proponent to introduce paragraph two because it is inadmissible character evidence.

5. Of the following:

    i.   A newspaper purporting to be the *New York Times*.

    ii. Law professor Bruce Bermer's curriculum vitae [résumé].

    iii. The label on a jar of Jif peanut butter.

    which are self-authenticating?

    A. None of them.

    B. i, but not ii or iii.

    C. ii, but not i or iii.

    D. iii, but not i or ii.

    E. i and ii, but not iii.

    F. i and iii, but not ii.

    G. ii and iii, but not i.

    H. All of them.

6. Next to each of the following, place a number from 1 to 4, using each number only once [in other words, no ties] with 1 meaning the conviction with the most likely chance of being allowed into evidence to impeach the witness ranging to 4 as the least likely.

    A. Three-year-old conviction for aggravated battery (punishable by imprisonment for three to five years) of a pure witness.

    B. Three-year-old conviction for aggravated battery (punishable by imprisonment for three to five years) of the accused after he testifies.

    C. Seventeen-year-old conviction for aggravated battery (punishable by imprisonment for three to five years) of a pure witness.

    D. Three-year-old conviction for fraud (punishable by imprisonment for one to eighteen months) of a pure witness.

7. Consider the three following propositions:

    i.   Someone says after an accident: "Whoa, pal, I'll give you $1,000 bucks, no questions asked, if you promise not to file a lawsuit. I ran the light and never saw you." His second sentence is admissible against him under the Federal Rules of Evidence to prove negligence.

    ii.   If P sues ABC Bus Company, P can, to show negligence of ABC's driver, Dan, introduce testimony that ABC fired Dan the following day.

    iii. The Federal Rules of Evidence contains a rule that a lawyer for either party is disqualified from being a witness in that case.

Which, if any, are true?

    A.   None of them.

    B.   i, but not ii or iii.

    C.   ii, but not i or iii.

    D.   iii, but not i or ii.

    E.   i and ii, but not iii.

    F.   i and iii, but not ii.

    G.   ii and iii, but not i.

    H.   All of them.

8.   When McCormick said "a brick is not a wall," he was making a point about how to understand the concept of:

    A.   hearsay;

    B.   character evidence;

    C.   impeachment;

    D.   relevancy;

    E.   masonry.

9.   Imagine a civil diversity action in the federal district court for the District of Nita in which all applicable state law would be based on the law of Nita. Assume also that Nita state law differs decisively from federal law in each of the following respects:

    i.   whether a particular hearsay declaration fits an exception to the hearsay rule;

    ii.   whether a particular communication between a doctor and a patient is privileged;

    iii. whether a particular evidentiary presumption is available to the plaintiff.

In which, if any, must the Court apply state law?

    A.   None of them.

    B.   i, but not ii or iii.

   C.   ii, but not i or iii.

   D.   iii, but not i or ii.

   E.   i and ii, but not iii.

   F.   i and iii, but not ii.

   G.   ii and iii, but not i.

   H.   All of them.

10. *P v. D.* P wants to introduce, to prove the matters asserted, salient sections of a speech given a month ago by Polly Tishun at a local political rally. X was present at that rally and heard the speech. Y was not present at the speech, but heard an audio recording of the lecture that Z had made and played for Y. P calls X and Y to testify to their recollections about what she said. D objects that such violates the original writing rule because P has made no proof that he is unable to produce an original of the recording. The court should:

   A.   Sustain the objection as to both witnesses.

   B.   Sustain the objection as to X, overrule it as to Y.

   C.   Overrule the objection as to X, sustain it as to Y.

   D.   Overrule the objection as to both witnesses.

11. Consider the following three propositions in connection with the civil trial, *P v. D*:

   i.   George Washington was the first President of the United States.

   ii.   The area of a circle is pi times the radius squared.

   iii. The traffic lights at the corner of Main and First Streets were not operating properly at 3:00 p.m. on October 16, 2008.

   Of which of the above must the Court, if requested, take judicial notice?

   A.   None of them.

   B.   i, but not ii or iii.

   C.   ii, but not i or iii.

   D.   iii, but not i or ii.

   E.   i and ii, but not iii.

F.   i and iii, but not ii.

G.   ii and iii, but not i.

H.   All of them.

12.   *Landlord v. Tenant* is an eviction action for violation of a rental agreement through intentional damage to the rental unit. Landlord calls W, who testifies that he saw Tenant punch a hole in a wall with his hand. On cross-examination, Tenant's counsel asks W, "Didn't you tell X the day after the event that you saw Landlord pick up Tenant and throw him at the wall and Tenant's hand went through the wall?" W says, "No, I said no such thing." Assume that Tenant has a witness, X, who would testify to Landlord's making this statement to him.

A.   Tenant cannot call the witness.

B.   Tenant may call the witness, but is not required to do so.

C.   Tenant must call the witness.

13.   Explain your last answer.

14.   Consider the following three allegations on appeal:

i.   The trial judge erred in deciding whether, on agreed-on facts, the admission of evidence violated the rules on character evidence.

ii.   The trial judge erred in permitting a question about an alleged prior dishonest act of the witness to be asked on cross-examination.

iii.   The trial judge erred when she determined a particular theory about psychology was sufficiently scientific to permit expert testimony.

As to which, if any, will the appellate court apply the de novo standard?

A.   None of them.

B.   i, but not ii or iii.

C.   ii, but not i or iii.

D.   iii, but not i or ii.

E.   i and ii, but not iii.

F.   i and iii, but not ii.

G.   ii and iii, but not i.

H.   All of them.

15. Consider the following ways to prove that a handwritten note was written by Arthur:

    i.   A lay witness recognizes Arthur's handwriting by prior familiarity.

    ii. A lay witness has been shown many exemplars of Arthur's handwriting and would state that the handwritten note was written by the same person that supplied the exemplars.

    iii. The note is signed "Arthur."

    Which are sufficient to authenticate the note as having been written by Arthur?

    A. None of them.

    B. i, but not ii or iii.

    C. ii, but not i or iii.

    D. iii, but not i or ii.

    E. i and ii, but not iii.

    F. i and iii, but not ii.

    G. ii and iii, but not i.

    H. All of them.

16. Consider the following three propositions:

    i.   A duplicate can never be admitted if an original is available.

    ii. An expert can never give an opinion on an ultimate issue.

    iii. No witness can testify without taking either an oath or affirmation.

    Which, if any, of these propositions are true?

    A. None of them.

    B. i, but not ii or iii.

    C. ii, but not i or iii.

    D. iii, but not i or ii.

    E. i and ii, but not iii.

    F. i and iii, but not ii.

    G. ii and iii, but not i.

    H. All of them.

17. *P v. D* is a suit to enforce a written contract. P has the burden of proving the terms of the contract. He has a duplicate of the contract, but all originals have been lost or destroyed through no fault of P. P also can produce F, the facilitator who enabled P and D to reach agreement and who wrote the contract for them in their presence. F has an excellent memory and could testify to the contents of the writing by that memory. Under the Federal Rules, P:

    A.   May not offer either the duplicate or F's testimony because only the original may be used to prove the contents of the writing.

    B.   Must offer the duplicate and may not offer F's testimony until he has introduced the duplicate.

    C.   Must offer F's testimony and may not offer the duplicate.

    D.   Must let D introduce a duplicate under Rule 106.

    E.   May offer either the duplicate or F's testimony.

18. Consider the following three preliminary statements:

    i.   A finding that an opinion from an expert witness will help the trier of fact before permitting the opinion's introduction.

    ii.   A finding that a piece of hearsay evidence fits an exception before it is admitted into evidence.

    iii. A finding that a handwriting was made by X before its relevance to the case.

    Assume that in each case the judge believes there is evidence "sufficient to support" the particular finding but is not persuaded of that finding by a preponderance of the evidence. In which situations, if any, should the judge permit the introduction of the evidence?

    A.   None of them.

    B.   i, but not ii or iii.

    C.   ii, but not i or iii.

    D.   iii, but not i or ii.

    E.   i and ii, but not iii.

    F.   i and iii, but not ii.

    G.   ii and iii, but not i.

    H.   All of them.

19. Consider the following three propositions found in different statutes:

    i.   If a person aims a gun at another person and shoots, then the jury may, but is not required to, find that the shooter had an intent to kill.

    ii.   If a person shows that he was injured by the negligence of a person driving a vehicle that carries letters or symbols indicating that the vehicle belongs to a company, then the company has the burden of persuading the jury that the driver either was not an employee or that the employee was not acting within the scope of his authority. If it does not so persuade the jury, it will be vicariously liable through respondeat superior for the injuries.

    iii. If a person shows that he mailed a properly addressed and stamped letter to recipient, then the jury must find that the recipient received it unless the recipient offers evidence of nonreceipt. If recipient does offer such evidence, the burden of persuasion remains on the alleged sender.

    Which of the above are "true presumptions?"

    A.   None of them.

    B.   i, but not ii or iii.

    C.   ii, but not i or iii.

    D.   iii, but not i or ii.

    E.   i and ii, but not iii.

    F.   i and iii, but not ii.

    G.   ii and iii, but not i.

    H.   All of them.

20. *P v. D* is an action to quiet title. During his case-in-chief, P offers paragraph one from a letter from a realtor, and paragraph one is admitted without objection. D requests the court to direct P to introduce paragraphs two and three from the same letter at this time. P objects and first notes that D could offer those paragraphs during D's case. P also objects that paragraph two is inadmissible hearsay. D notes that paragraph one contains the exact same inadmissible hearsay. P notes that paragraph three violates the rule on character evidence, which neither paragraph one nor two do. The court finds that all of these arguments are true. The court should:

    A.   Wait until D's case to permit the introduction of anything beyond paragraph one.

    B.   Direct P to introduce both paragraphs two and three.

    C.   Direct P to introduce paragraph two, but not paragraph three.

    D.   Direct P to introduce paragraph three, but not paragraph two.

21. Consider the following three methods for proving that a voice heard on an incoming phone call was Cynthia's voice:

    i.   The call's recipient recognized Cynthia's voice because he has talked to Cynthia on many occasions both on the phone and in person.

    ii.   The caller identified herself as Cynthia.

    iii. The caller relayed information that only Cynthia could have had.

    Which of the above, by itself, would be sufficient to authenticate the voice as Cynthia's?

    A.   None of them.

    B.   i, but not ii or iii.

    C.   ii, but not i or iii.

    D.   iii, but not i or ii.

    E.   i and ii, but not iii.

    F.   i and iii, but not ii.

    G.   ii and iii, but not i.

    H.   All of them.

22. The defendant in a civil case may impeach:

    A.   Only witnesses called by the plaintiff.

    B.   Only witnesses called by the defendant.

    C.   Witnesses called by either party.

    D.   Only hostile witnesses.

    E.   Only witnesses whose testimony meets the "surprise and affirmative damage" test.

23. Of the following:

    i.   a certified copy of a public record,

    ii. a certified copy of a business record of a private company,

    iii. a newspaper purporting to be the *Chicago Tribune*,

which are self-authenticating?

    A. None of them.

    B. i, but not ii or iii.

    C. ii, but not i or iii.

    D. iii, but not i or ii.

    E. i and ii, but not iii.

    F. i and iii, but not ii.

    G. ii and iii, but not i.

    H. All of them.

24. *State v. Dilbert*, a criminal prosecution for theft. Dilbert calls Al Ibby, who would testify that Dilbert was with him in another city at the time of the theft. The prosecution wants to impeach Al with a conviction for the crime of aggravated battery. The conviction took place twelve years ago, and Al thereafter spent four years in prison subsequent to the conviction. Dilbert objects. The court should:

    A. Allow the evidence without any balancing.

    B. Allow the evidence if its probative value substantially outweighs its prejudicial effect.

    C. Allow the evidence if its probative value outweighs its prejudicial effect.

    D. Allow the evidence unless its prejudicial effect substantially outweighs its probative value.

    E. Not allow the evidence under any circumstances.

25. Consider the following three propositions:

    i. The presiding judge at a trial may never testify as a witness in that trial.

    ii. The fact that someone does or does not have liability insurance is never admissible.

    iii. If someone after an accident says, "Here's $500 toward your injuries; I'm sorry for driving through the stop sign," his second sentence is admissible against him under the Federal Rules of Evidence.

Which, if any, of these propositions are true?

    A. None of them.

    B. i, but not ii or iii.

    C.   ii, but not i or iii.

    D.   iii, but not i or ii.

    E.   i and ii, but not iii.

    F.   i and iii, but not ii.

    G.   ii and iii, but not i.

    H.   All of them.

26.   The lawyer-client privilege is owned by:

    A.   The lawyer.

    B.   The client.

    C.   The lawyer and the client.

    D.   Bill Gates.

27.   *Pablo v. Delores*, a negligence action involving a collision between Delores' car and Pablo's motorcycle. Pablo calls Loren Awda, the police officer who was called to the scene of the accident. After testifying to what he saw, Pablo's attorney hands Loren a photograph and the following dialogue occurs:

Attorney: Do you recognize the photograph?

Loren: Yes, that's the scene about ten minutes after the accident and just as I arrived. It shows Pablo and his motorcycle in the road.

Attorney: Did you take this photograph?

Loren: No.

Attorney: Do you know who did?

Loren: Not really. There was a guy there from the local paper, and he had a camera guy with him. Maybe he took it. I really don't know.

Attorney: Does it accurately depict the scene.

Loren: It sure does.

The attorney offers the photograph. Delores's counsel objects on all grounds shown below. The photograph is:

    A.   Inadmissible because it is cumulative—the officer has already described the scene verbally.

    B.   Inadmissible because the photograph has not been authenticated.

C.   Inadmissible because the photograph violates the Original Writing rule.

D.   Inadmissible because the photograph is inadmissible hearsay.

E.   Inadmissible under Rule 403.

F.   Admissible.

28.   Consider the following three alleged errors:

i.   The judge erred in finding that three seconds was the maximum amount of delay between event and statement for an excited utterance.

ii.   The judge erred in believing P's witness, X, instead of D's witness, Y, on a controverted fact preliminary to excluding evidence.

iii.   The judge erred in not allowing the impeachment of P's witness, Z, through a two-year-old conviction for perjury.

On appeal, to which of the above events will the standard of de novo review be applied?

A.   None of them.

B.   i, but not ii or iii.

C.   ii, but not i or iii.

D.   iii, but not i or ii.

E.   i and ii, but not iii.

F.   i and iii, but not ii.

G.   ii and iii, but not i.

H.   All of them.

29.   Landowner and Merchant enter into a rental contract for premises in the business district. The contract consists not of a single document, but of a series of letters passing between Landowner and Merchant that set the terms. A dispute develops about the contract's meaning, and both parties hire Mediator to try to settle the dispute. Mediator asks each party to write a summary of his arguments of what the language was intended to mean. The parties give those summaries and the series of letters to Mediator. The mediation does not produce a solution. Landowner sues Merchant. Landowner wants to introduce into evidence both the letters that constitute the contract and the written summaries. The court should:

A.   Admit neither the letters nor the summaries.

B.   Admit the letters, but not the summaries.

    C.   Admit the summaries, but not the letters.

    D.   Admit both the letters and the summaries.

30. Consider the following three propositions in connection with a civil trial in Nita County [Nita City, largest city in the State of Nita, is the county seat of Nita County]:

    i.   The main street in Nita is The Way of the Righteous.

    ii.   The human voice operates between 200 hertz and 800 hertz.

    iii. The earth revolves around the sun.

Of which of the above must the court, if requested, take judicial notice?

    A.   None of them.

    B.   i, but not ii or iii.

    C.   ii, but not i or iii.

    D.   iii, but not i or ii.

    E.   i and ii, but not iii.

    F.   i and iii, but not ii.

    G.   ii and iii, but not i.

    H.   All of them.

31. Consider the following three alleged trial errors:

    i.   The judge erred in determining whether a given communication was privileged.

    ii.   The judge erred in determining whether, in a civil case, judicial notice should have been taken of a particular fact.

    iii. The judge erred in determining whether it was proper to ask a witness on cross-examination, "Isn't it true that two weeks ago you defrauded a customer?"

To which will an appellate court apply a de novo standard of review?

    A.   None of them.

    B.   i, but not ii or iii.

    C.   ii, but not i or iii.

D. iii, but not i or ii.

E. i and ii, but not iii.

F. i and iii, but not ii.

G. ii and iii, but not i.

H. All of them.

32. *State v. Doug* is a prosecution for robbery. Prosecution offers testimony from Doug's wife. Doug objects that the testimony would breach the marital communication privilege. When determining whether it is privileged, what standard must the judge apply?

A. A scintilla of evidence.

B. Evidence sufficient to support a finding.

C. Preponderance of the evidence.

D. Beyond a reasonable doubt.

33. Consider the following preliminary statements:

i. A finding that a lay witness's opinion is helpful to the jury.

ii. A finding that a damaged sofa in a photograph is the sofa belonging to P that D spilled acid on, before admitting the photograph.

iii. A finding that an expert's opinion is based on a sufficiently scientific principle.

Assume that in each case, the judge believes that there is "evidence sufficient to support a finding" that the preliminary fact is true, but not a "preponderance of the evidence." In which case(s), if any, should the judge admit the proffered evidence?

A. None of them.

B. i, but not ii or iii.

C. ii, but not i or iii.

D. iii, but not i or ii.

E. i and ii, but not iii.

F. i and iii, but not ii.

G. ii and iii, but not i.

H. All of them.

34. P and D try to settle their dispute about P's injuries in a car accident by using a mediator. The following all occur, among other things, at the mediation hearing:

    i. D introduces a report that he prepared for the mediation.

    ii. D states that he probably was speeding when he hit P.

    iii. D enters a copy of the police report of the accident.

    The mediation is unsuccessful, and P sues D. At the trial, D objects to the introduction of each of the above based on Rule 408. The judge should grant that motion for:

    A. None of them.

    B. i, but not ii or iii.

    C. ii, but not i or iii.

    D. iii, but not i or ii.

    E. i and ii, but not iii.

    F. i and iii, but not ii.

    G. ii and iii, but not i.

    H. All of them.

35. *State v. Raser* is a prosecution for speeding. Raser is charged with doing forty miles per hour in a twenty-five-mile-per-hour zone. State calls Officer Guy Vieux, a thirty-year veteran of the force, to testify that he was sitting by the side of the road watching traffic, that his radar was not working that day, and that he saw Raser go by doing, in Vieux's opinion, "at least fifty miles per hour." Raser objects that this is an inadmissible opinion. The court should:

    A. Exclude the testimony as speculation.

    B. Exclude the testimony because speed is an ultimate issue in a speeding case.

    C. Exclude the opinion unless Vieux is first qualified as an expert.

    D. Admit the testimony as helpful lay opinion.

36. *State v. Dudley* involves a bank robbery. The robber, wearing a ski mask, handed a handwritten note to the teller, which said, "Putt all the money in the bagg and you won'tt gett hurtt." After the teller gave money to the robber, he

fled and left the note behind. Consider the following possible ways to prove that Dudley wrote the note:

i.   A longtime acquaintance of Dudley recognizes the handwriting as Dudley's.

ii. A former teacher of Dudley's would state that Dudley had "an incredibly odd tendency" to double all ending consonants when he wrote.

iii. The note was signed, "Dudley."

Which, by itself, could be sufficient to authenticate the note as having been written by Dudley?

A.   None of them.

B.   i, but not ii or iii.

C.   ii, but not i or iii.

D.   iii, but not i or ii.

E.   i and ii, but not iii.

F.   i and iii, but not ii.

G.   ii and iii, but not i.

H.   All of them.

37. *P v. D* is a contract case. P wants to prove the content of a writing. Through no fault of his own, he does not have an original of the writing, but does have a duplicate. Instead of introducing the duplicate, he wants to testify from his memory about the content. He can do so:

A.   Under neither the "American" nor the "British" approach.

B.   Under the "American," but not the "British," approach.

C.   Under the "British," but not the "American," approach.

D.   Under either the "American" or the "British" approach.

38. Which of the following are "true presumptions:"

i.   A statute that provides: "In any situation in which the payee has possession of a negotiable instrument signed by a maker or drawer, it shall be presumed that the maker or drawer delivered the instrument to the payee, and the maker or drawer shall not be permitted to introduce any evidence to the contrary."

ii. A judge-made rule that states: "If a person aims a deadly weapon at another person and pulls the trigger, the jury may presume that the person did so with the intent to kill."

iii. A statute that provides: "If the plaintiff proves that defendant's action had the effect of discriminating against him, the burden of disproving the intention of discriminating will be shifted to the defendant."

    A. None of them.

    B. i, but not ii or iii.

    C. ii, but not i or iii.

    D. iii, but not i or ii.

    E. i and ii, but not iii.

    F. i and iii, but not ii.

    G. ii and iii, but not i.

    H. All of them.

39. Consider the following propositions:

    i. Water freezes at zero degrees Celsius.

    ii. Nita City is in the State of Nita.

    iii. James Madison was the fourth President of the United States.

In a civil trial in Nita City, Nita, as to which of the above must the court give judicial notice if requested?

    A. None of them.

    B. i, but not ii or iii.

    C. ii, but not i or iii.

    D. iii, but not i or ii.

    E. i and ii, but not iii.

    F. i and iii, but not ii.

    G. ii and iii, but not i.

    H. All of them.

40. A's car and B's car collide in an intersection. A says to B: "If you promise not to sue me, I'll give you $500 to call it even. My guess is that I went through a red light." B says to A: "I'll not accept anything. This whole thing was my fault. I'll send you a check for $1,000." The check is, of course, never sent. A sues B, and B counterclaims. A offers B's statement. B offers A's statement. The court should:

    A. Allow neither statement.

    B. Allow A to introduce B's statement, but not allow B to introduce A's statement.

    C. Allow B to introduce A's statement, but not allow A to introduce B's statement.

    D. Allow both statements.

41. *State v. Dave* is a criminal trial for robbery. Dave confessed, but the confession was suppressed prior to trial as violative of the Fifth Amendment and *Miranda*. Dave is convicted. Dave's lawyer learns several weeks later, when he runs into a juror on the street, that during deliberations, the bailiff told the jurors that Dave had confessed, but that they didn't get to hear it in the courtroom because some "tricky lawyer" found a "technical" problem with it. Dave files a motion to set aside the verdict and wants to call this juror and offer this testimony. The court should:

    A. Not permit this because a juror cannot impeach his own verdict.

    B. Not permit this because this is harmless error.

    C. Not permit this because a juror cannot be called as a witness.

    D. Permit this.

42. *P v. D* is a personal injury case. To prove that D ran the red light, P offered the testimony of X—that he was facing away from the street and conversing with Y, who was looking at the street, and that just as X heard a crash, Y's eyes opened wide and Y said, "Wow, that blue car just ran straight through the red light!" The court permitted this testimony. During D's case-in-chief, D offers a certified copy of an eight-year-old conviction of Y for perjury. The court should:

    A. Admit the conviction for impeachment purposes.

    B. Exclude the conviction as hearsay.

    C.   Exclude the conviction because the impeachment of Y is inappropriate.

    D.   Exclude the conviction based on the Original Writing Rule.

43. Consider which, if any, of the following questions are leading questions when asked on direct examination to a non-hostile, non-adverse witness.

    i.   "Did you go there at 7:00?"

    ii. "Isn't it true that you sneaked out before this happened?"

    iii. "You stated that he returned home that night. Do you remember what time he returned?"

    A.   None of them.

    B.   i, but not ii or iii.

    C.   ii, but not i or iii.

    D.   iii, but not i or ii.

    E.   i and ii, but not iii.

    F.   i and iii, but not ii.

    G.   ii and iii, but not i.

    H.   All of them.

44. Which of the following preliminary statements need only satisfy the lesser standard, "sufficient to support a finding"?

    i.   In a case involving the Original Writing Rule, whether the asserted writing ever existed.

    ii. Whether a statement is or is not offered to prove the "truth of the matter asserted."

    iii. Whether an item sought to be introduced is what the proponent claims it to be.

    A.   None of them.

    B.   i, but not ii or iii.

    C.   ii, but not i or iii.

    D.   iii, but not i or ii.

E.   i and ii, but not iii.

F.   i and iii, but not ii.

G.   ii and iii, but not i.

H.   All of them.

45.   Assume a civil diversity action in federal district court. Assume that for each of the following, the federal rule differs decisively from the rule of the state in which the action is located:

i.   Whether a hearsay statement does or does not fit an exception.

ii.   Whether a statement is privileged as a marital communication.

iii. Whether a document is sufficiently authenticated.

In which should the court apply state law?

A.   None of them.

B.   i, but not ii or iii.

C.   ii, but not i or iii.

D.   iii, but not i or ii.

E.   i and ii, but not iii.

F.   i and iii, but not ii.

G.   ii and iii, but not i.

H.   All of them.

SECTION B(3)

TRIAL SCENARIO PROBLEMS

ALL BOUND FOR MORNINGTOWN

Clin, Gluren, and Knik, all neurologists, formed a closely held corporation, "Sleep Laboratories, Inc.," to administer polysomnograms and other medical procedures to examine patients for sleep disorders. Business had recently boomed in their sleepy community, and they had begun the process of issuing stock to the public to raise a large amount of capital for labs in other cities. About two months into this process, Clin was discovered dead in his bed at home. According to the medical examiner, the cause of death was "suffocation during sleep." After a police investigation, Gluren was arrested and charged with the first-degree murder of Clin.

At the trial, the State calls Knik, who would testify that Clin, Gluren, and Knik had seriously misrepresented much of the information that they released to the public concerning their business [you should assume that such would violate a federal criminal statute]. Knik would further testify that a week before his death, Clin had called a meeting of the three of them and said that he was beginning to lose sleep over their wrongdoing and was considering going to federal authorities to alert them to the scam.

1. **Gluren objects that such would be improper character evidence? What result and why? [Please at this point ignore any hearsay issue.]**

2. **Assuming the prior objection is overruled, Gluren now objects that the testimony of what was said at the meeting would violate the hearsay rule. What result and why?**

The prosecution has evidence that twenty-five years ago, Gluren, before he went to medical school, was a partner in an auto junkyard business, "Gluren and Puanteur," and was convicted for the aggravated battery of his partner, Puanteur, and sentenced to two years in prison. The prosecutor notified Gluren well in advance of the trial that she would offer this evidence during her case-in-chief.

3. **What is the prosecutor's best argument for admissibility, and should it be admitted?**

When Clin was found dead, the area around his bed was searched by police, and fingerprints other than Clin's were found on four items near the bed. The prints were sent to the state crime lab, which issued a report indicating that the prints found in the room matched prints on record for Gluren. Prosecution offers the report.

4. **Assuming defendant makes the best objection, how should the court rule and why?**

After he was arrested, Gluren was interrogated by city police Toody and Muldoon and given *Miranda* warnings. Toody said, "You help us out, and we'll put in a word for you with the prosecutor." Gluren said, "OK, I was in his house that night, but that's all I'm going to tell you."

5. **Prosecution calls Officer Toody to testify to this exchange of statements. Gluren objects based on Rule 410. What result and why?**

6. **Prosecution next calls Songeur, another neurologist, who would testify that he knows Gluren's reputation in the community and that Gluren is well known to be a volatile and violent person. Gluren objects. What result and why?**

Prosecution next calls Apnea, Gluren's wife, to testify that she saw Gluren leave their house at midnight on the night in question and return about 1:30 a.m. Apnea is willing to testify. Gluren objects based on "the marital privilege." Assume that the state law on the marital privileges is the same in this state as in the federal system.

7. **How should the court rule and why?**

Prosecution next calls Augen who testifies that he saw Gluren walking out of Clin's house the night of the murder. On cross-examination, Gluren's lawyer asks Augen, "Isn't it a fact that you over-reported your expenses to your employer last month?"

8. **Prosecution objects that this is improper cross-examination. What result and why?**

Assume now that this question is permitted and that Augen denies it. Prosecution rests and defense opens its case-in-chief. Defense calls C. Pap, Augen's employer, who would testify that indeed Augen over-reported his expenses last month at work.

9. **Prosecution objects. What result and why?**

Defense next calls Assonnato, who says he has known Gluren for many years and that most recently he saw Gluren at Assonnato's birthday party at Cal's Bar and Grill. Assonnato would testify that in his opinion, Gluren is a peaceful person. Prosecution objects that such is improper character evidence.

10. **How should the court rule and why?**

Assume Assonnato is permitted to testify. For impeachment purposes, prosecution wants to offer a conviction of Assonnato for rape. The conviction was twelve years ago, and Assonnato served five years in prison. Gluren objects that this is improper impeachment.

11. **What standard should the court apply in deciding whether to permit this conviction for impeachment purposes?**

On cross-examination of Assonnato, prosecution asks, "Isn't it true that you told Blain Wave that you most recently saw Gluren at your birthday party at Jerry's Bar and Grill?" Gluren objects that this is improper cross-examination.

12. **How should the court rule and why?**

After defense rests, prosecution during its case in rebuttal calls Blain Wave to testify that Assonnato told him he saw Gluren at his party at Jerry's Bar and Grill, not Cal's. Gluren objects.

13. **How should the court rule and why?**

Prosecution calls Songeur to testify that Clin has a reputation for being a peaceful person.

14. **How should the court rule and why?**

The prosecution asks the court to instruct the jury during final instructions based on this recently passed Nita State statute: "In all criminal cases, upon proof that defendant has committed an act that produced death, the jury shall presume that such was done intentionally unless the defendant persuades the jury by a preponderance of the evidence that such intent was lacking." Gluren objects.

15. **How should the court rule and why?**

Don't Chute!!

Paul Novizio v. Dave's Sky-Diving School, Inc. and Eddie Addetto is a negligence action for injuries Paul suffered on the first day of his instruction in skydiving when his parachute did not completely open. Paul claims that the school, through its employees, including Eddie, was negligent. Dave's alleges, among other things, that Paul was contributorily negligent.

Before the first witness is called, Paul asks the court to exclude all witnesses except for parties and their representatives from the courtroom until they testify. Dave's and Eddie object.

1. How should the court rule and why?

To prove Dave's is careless, Paul calls Walt Vidne to testify that Walt was hurt last year by the negligence of Dave's in a similar situation and that Dave's settled with Walt for $100,000 for his injuries. Dave's objects.

2. What is Dave's best objection, and how should the court rule?

Paul next calls I. Oeil, who testifies about the incident that produced Paul's injuries. On cross-examination, Dave's attorney asks Oeil, "Isn't it true that you intentionally misrecorded your scores on three holes in last weekend's pro-am golf tournament and were caught?" Paul objects that this is improper cross-examination.

3. How should the court rule and why?

Assume that the court permits the question and that Oeil denies it. Part of Oeil's direct testimony was that Paul was very careful in what he was doing at the time he was hurt. Dave's attorney asks Oeil on cross-examination, "Isn't it true that a day after the accident, you told your friend, Fred Copain, that Paul was clowning around in a reckless way when he was hurt?" Paul objects that this is improper cross-examination.

4. How should the court rule and why?

Assume that the question is allowed and that Oeil denies having made any such statement. Paul next calls Father Flanagan, the priest of Eddie Addetto (who was present when Paul was hurt), to testify that Eddie confessed to Father Flanagan at confession that Eddie hurt Paul through carelessness. Eddie objects.

5. What is the best objection, and how should the court rule?

Paul next calls Parry Fallschirm and qualifies him as an expert in skydiving and in parachute design and packing. Parry, who examined the chute that Paul used, would testify that the chute was improperly packed for Paul's jump. Dave's objects that such would be testimony about an ultimate issue for the jury and is thus improper.

6. How should the court rule and why?

Paul next calls Stanley Renifleur, who would testify that he has determined that improperly packed parachutes give off an unusual odor that properly packed chutes do not, that he smelled the pack the day following the accident, and that it gave off this odor.

7. What is Dave's best objection to this evidence?

After several other witnesses, Paul rests his case. Dave's opens its case by calling Herb Tanteador, the official scorer at last week's golf tournament that Oeil [who testified for Paul] participated in, to testify that Oeil indeed was caught trying to turn in false golf scores from his round. Paul objects.

8. How should the court rule and why?

Dave's next calls Fred Copain to testify that a day after the accident, Oeil told Fred [remember that Oeil has denied this] that Paul was clowning around in a reckless way when he was hurt to prove that such statement was true.

9. What is Paul's best objection, and how should the court rule?

Assume now that the court did not permit the testimony for that purpose. Dave's now proffers the same statement to impeach Oeil.

10. How should the court rule and why?

Dave's next calls one of its employees who was present that day, Willy Workman, to testify to what he saw when the injury occurred. Paul objects noting that Willy Workman is employed by Dave's, is thus biased, and should be ruled not competent for that reason.

11. How should the court rule and why?

Assume the court permits Willy to testify. Willy is asked on direct to estimate the speed at which Paul was traveling when he landed during his "lesson jump," when the parachute was not completely open.

12. What kinds of questions should Dave's counsel ask first to improve the chances that the court will permit this testimony?

Dave's next calls Jerry Wertend to testify that Parry Fallschirm [who testified for Paul], in Jerry's opinion, is a very untruthful person. Paul argues that Parry's character has not been put in issue and that the question is therefore improper.

13. How should the court rule and why?

Assume the court allows the testimony and that Jerry states that, in his opinion, Parry is a very untruthful person and that, indeed, he has a reputation for being dishonest. Dave's attorney then asks, "Could you give us an example of this untruthfulness, please?" Paul's lawyer objects.

14. How should the court rule and why?